MEN AND WOMEN OF PROVERBS

By Scott Hanks, Ph.D.

About the Author

Dr. Scott Hanks was born near Chicago, Illinois and had the unique opportunity of growing up in a preacher's home. Being brought up in a Christian home with parents who put an emphasis on living for the Lord, gave him a good foundation for what he preaches and teaches today.

After completing his education in a Christian high school, Dr. Scott Hanks attended Bible college, where he earned his Bachelor of Science and Masters degrees in Education. He would later earn his Ph.D. in 2007.

He served as an assistant pastor and Christian school teacher for five years in Sauk Village, Illinois under the leadership of his father, Dr. John A. Hanks. In 1994, the Lord led Dr. Scott Hanks and his wife Stacia, to Lawrence, Kansas where he continues to pastor the Heritage Baptist Church. The Lord has blessed their home with six children, Sharon, Seth, Samuel, Silas, Stephen, and Stephanie.

He has authored many other titles in addition to *Men and Women of Proverbs.* Other books include devotion books, discipleship material, Sunday school curriculum, and many books for Christian growth.

Recommendation

Scott Hanks is a one-of-a-kind man who has written a one-of-a-kind book. We know as believers that God's wisdom from above is the only wisdom worth guiding our lives by.

I have other books on my shelf written about Proverbs, including one book which categorizes the different men and subjects of Proverbs. But nowhere in existence have I ever seen a division of Proverbs which is so resourceful in that it gives the examples of these types of men in the margin of the page. It is almost like having a volume of assembled wisdom or to preachers it is like having a volume of assembled messages.

What an excellent tool for a Wednesday night Bible study, or for a devotion time with the family in moving through each of the "Men of Proverbs", relating the Scriptures, and pointing out the illustrations in the men they represent in other places in the Bible. What a great study on a personal basis to enrich and increase our wisdom.

I highly recommend this book to all who would like a very rich resource for Bible profit and enjoyment.

Pastor Larry Brown
Marion Avenue Baptist Church
Washington, Iowa

TABLE OF CONTENTS

The Men of Proverbs

The Women of Proverbs

Contrasting Men

The Foolish Man ....The Wise Man

The Scornful Man........................The Wise Man

The Simple Man.................The Prudent Man

The Slothful Man .... The Diligent Man

The Poor Man ....The Rich Man

The Wicked Man............................The Just Man

The Wicked Man.............The Righteous Man

The Young Man ....The Old Man

The Evil Man............................The Good Man

The Angry Man .... The Discreet Man

The Froward Man .... The Upright Man

Contrasting Women

The Evil Woman ....The God-Fearing Woman

The Strange Woman....................... The Virtuous Woman

The Foolish Woman............................ The Wise Woman

Introduction

My love for the book of Proverbs began in my teen years when I was encouraged to read a chapter in Proverbs every day. I was impressed with its wealth of practical truths and soon began word and verse studies using my Bible and a concordance. It is from these studies that the majority of this book was written, although I did not begin the studies with the idea of writing a book. I merely studied for my personal devotions and growth as a Christian, and quickly found that the value of Proverbs is immeasurable and the end of its truths unreachable.

Through the years, wisdom has been defined in many different ways, one of those being to "see things the way God sees them." The book of Proverbs clearly defines how God sees man! In the *Men and Women of Proverbs*, each type of person is defined and their distinctive characteristics and actions are listed. The reader can picture himself as God sees him and make the necessary changes to become the wise Christian God desires for him to be. May God bless each person who studies Proverbs!

Pastor Scott Hanks

Study Guide

Using the Men and Women of Proverbs, a Christian can look at the characteristics of each man and decide which ones should or should not be copied. There is also a Bible character listed that best illustrates the actions and characteristics of each man. By studying the stories of the Bible characters, we can see the qualities we need to develop to be godly Christians.

Since its first printing, many churches have found this book helpful in the following ways:

1. Sunday School Lessons
2. Midweek Bible Studies
3. Christian School Bible Class Curriculum
4. Family Devotion Resource
5. Youth Group Challenges
6. Sermon Outlines
7. Personal Bible Study
8. Staff Devotions
9. Group Bible Study

The easy-to-read format lends itself to many uses. The basic thoughts and outlines are in the book and can be as simple or detailed as needed.

All scripture is from the King James Bible. References used include <u>Noah Webster's 1828 Dictionary</u> and <u>Strong's Exhaustive Concordance</u>.

Chapter 1

THE FOOLISH MAN

Proverbs 14:7
Go from the presence of a foolish man,
when thou perceivest not in
him the lips of knowledge.

The Wise Man's opposite is the Foolish Man. Their characteristics are distinctly different. In the New Testament, the fool is a lost man. Christians have the ability to "act" foolish as well. This is simply done by taking on the actions of the lost.

The Foolish Man's life can be summed up in one verse. Proverbs 12:15 says, "The way of a fool is right in his own eyes . . ." He has all the answers and needs no one else's opinions. He does not care what others may think about him and is certainly apathetic concerning God's attitude toward him. He is not willing to learn from anyone; he knows it all already. When he opens his mouth, he reveals his folly.

God warns against spending time with such a man. His ungodly traits may rub off. Foolish Men are easy to spot. They are not worth any effort of befriending. It is a waste of time and perhaps a waste of a life to spend time with such a character (Proverbs 14:7).

The inevitable end of the Foolish Man is death and destruction. Unfortunately, before this, the fool must undergo much correction and heartache. A Christian must determine to stay away from Foolish Men and refrain from foolish actions.

The Foolish Man

Dictionary "FOOL": One who is destitute of reason. One who follows his own inclinations.

Hebrew "FOOL": Fat, stupid or silly (3684)

I.   Actions of the Foolish Man
A.   Despises Wisdom

Rehoboam
I Kings 12:8

1.   The fear of the LORD is the beginning of know-ledge: but fools despise wisdom and instruction. Proverbs 1:7
2.   Wherefore is there a price in the hand of a fool to get wisdom, seeing he hath no heart to it? Proverbs 17:16
3.   Wisdom is before him that hath understanding; but the eyes of a fool are in the ends of the earth. Proverbs 17:24
4.   Speak not in the ears of a fool: for he will despise the wisdom of thy words. Proverbs 23:9
5.   Wisdom is too high for a fool: he openeth not his mouth in the gate. Proverbs 24:7

B.   Despises Instruction

Children
of Israel
II Kings 17:14

1.   The fear of the LORD is the beginning of know-ledge: but fools despise wisdom and instruction. Proverbs 1:7
2.   A fool despiseth his father's instruction: but he that regardeth reproof is prudent. Proverbs 15:5

C. Hates Knowledge

Jeroboam
I Kings 13:1-5

1. How long, ye simple ones, will ye love simplicity? and the scorners delight in their scorning, and fools hate knowledge? Proverbs 1:22
2. The lips of the wise disperse knowledge: but the heart of the foolish doeth not so. Proverbs 15:7

D. Grieves His Mother

Esau
Genesis 26:34, 35

1. The proverbs of Solomon. A wise son maketh a glad father: but a foolish son is the heaviness of his mother. Proverbs 10:1
2. A wise son maketh a glad father: but a foolish man despiseth his mother. Proverbs 15:20
3. A foolish son is a grief to his father, and bitterness to her that bare him. Proverbs 17:25

E. Flatters People, Who Inside, He Truly Hates

Sanballat
Nehemiah 6:2

He that hideth hatred with lying lips, and he that uttereth a slander, is a fool. Proverbs 10:18

F. Slanders

Tobiah
Nehemiah 4:1-3

He that hideth hatred with lying lips, and he that uttereth slander, is a fool. Proverbs 10:18

11

G. Laughs at Sin

Samson
Judges 16:1-17

1. It is as sport to a fool to do mischief: but a man of understanding hath wisdom. Proverbs 10:23
2. Fools make a mock at sin: but among the righteous there is favour. Proverbs 14:9
3. Folly is joy to him that is destitute of wisdom: but a man of understanding walketh uprightly. Proverbs 15:21

H. Lets His Wrath Be Known

Balaam
Numbers 22:27

1. A fool's wrath is presently known: but a prudent man covereth shame. Proverbs 12:16
2. He that is soon angry dealeth foolishly: and a man of wicked devices is hated. Proverbs 14:17

I. Speaks Foolishness

Cain
Genesis 4:6-10

1. A prudent man concealeth knowledge: but the heart of fools proclaimeth foolishness. Proverbs 12:23
2. The tongue of the wise useth knowledge aright: but the mouth of fools poureth out foolishness. Proverbs 15:2

J. Is Not Ashamed of His Foolishness

Amnon
II Samuel 13:12-14

1. Every prudent man dealeth with knowledge: but a fool layeth open his folly. Proverbs 13:16
2. The heart of him that hath understanding seeketh knowledge: but the mouth of fools feedeth on foolishness. Proverbs 15:14

K. Does Evil

Haman
Esther 3:6-10

1. The desire accomplished is sweet to the soul: but it is abomination to fools to depart from evil. Proverbs 13:19
2. A wise man feareth, and departeth from evil: but the fool rageth, and is confident. Proverbs 14:16

L. Tells All He Knows

Doeg
I Samuel 22:9, 10

1. Wisdom resteth in the heart of him that hath understanding: but that which is in the midst of fools is made known. Proverbs 14:33
2. A fool uttereth all his mind: but a wise man keepeth it in till afterwards. Proverbs 29:11

M. Rejects Reproof

Hophni and
Phinehas
I Samuel 2:23-25

A reproof entereth more into a wise man than an hundred stripes into a fool. Proverbs 17:10

13

N. Disappoints His Father

Absalom
II Samuel 13:37; 18:33

1. He that begetteth a fool doeth it to his sorrow: and the father of a fool hath no joy. Proverbs 17:21
2. A foolish son is a grief to his father, and bitterness to her that bare him. Proverbs 17:25
3. A foolish son is the calamity of his father: and the contentions of a wife are a continual dropping. Proverbs 19:13

O. Lacks Understanding

Rich Young Ruler
Mark 10:17-22

1. Wisdom resteth in the heart of him that hath understanding: but that which is in the midst of fools is made known. Proverbs 14:33
2. Wisdom is before him that hath understanding; but the eyes of a fool are in the ends of the earth. Proverbs 17:24
3. A fool hath no delight in understanding, but that his heart may discover itself. Proverbs 18:2

P. Speaks without Thought

Herod (The Great)
Matthew 14:6-9

1. He that answereth a matter before he heareth it, it is folly and shame unto him. Proverbs 18:13
2. Seest thou a man that is hasty in his words? there is more hope of a fool than of him. Proverbs 29:20

Q. Speaks Perversely

Shimei
II Samuel 16:5-7

> Better is the poor that walketh in his integrity, than he that is perverse in his lips, and is a fool. Proverbs 19:1

R. Is Repeatedly Foolish

Adonijah
I Kings 2:22-25

> As a dog returneth to his vomit, so a fool returneth to his folly. Proverbs 26:11

II. Characteristics of a Foolish Man
A. Does What Is Right in His Eyes

Children
of Israel
Judges 17:6; 21:25

1. The way of a fool is right in his own eyes: but he that hearkeneth unto counsel is wise. Proverbs 12:15
2. He that trusteth in his own heart is a fool: but whoso walketh wisely, he shall be delivered. Proverbs 28:26

B. Is Soon Angry (Temper)

Nebuchadnezzar
Daniel 3:13

1. He that is soon angry dealeth foolishly: and a man of wicked devices is hated. Proverbs 14:17
2. It is an honour for a man to cease from strife: but

every fool will be meddling. Proverbs 20:3

3. A stone is heavy, and the sand weighty; but a fool's wrath is heavier than them both. Proverbs 27:3

C. Is Proud

Saul
I Samuel 15:1-17

1. In the mouth of the foolish is a rod of pride: but the lips of the wise shall preserve them. Proverbs 14:3
2. If thou hast done foolishly in lifting up thyself, or if thou hast thought evil, lay thine hand upon thy mouth. Proverbs 30:32

D. Is Deceitful

Judas
John 6:70, 71

The wisdom of the prudent is to understand his way: but the folly of fools is deceit. Proverbs 14:8

E. Is Wasteful

Unjust Steward
Luke 16:1

There is treasure to be desired and oil in the dwelling of the wise; but a foolish man spendeth it up. Proverbs 21:20

III. Consequences of the Foolish Man
A. Receives Shame
The wise shall inherit glory: but shame shall be the promotion of fools. Proverbs 3:35
B. Receives Correction

He goeth after her straightway, as an ox goeth to the slaughter, or as a fool to the correction of the stocks; Proverbs 7:22

C. Falls

1. The wise in heart will receive commandments: but a prating fool shall fall. Proverbs 10:8
2. He that winketh with the eye causeth sorrow: but a prating fool shall fall. Proverbs 10:10

D. Is Destroyed

1. Wise men lay up knowledge: but the mouth of the foolish is near destruction. Proverbs 10:14
2. He that walketh with wise men shall be wise: but a companion of fools shall be destroyed. Proverbs 13:20
3. A fool's mouth is his destruction, and his lips are the snare of his soul. Proverbs 18:7

E. Dies

The lips of the righteous feed many: but fools die for want of wisdom. Proverbs 10:21

F. Serves

He that troubleth his own house shall inherit the wind: and the fool shall be servant to the wise of heart. Proverbs 11:29

G. Brings Contention

A fool's lips enter into contention, and his mouth calleth for strokes. Proverbs 18:6

H. Has No Delight

1. Delight is not seemly for a fool; much less for a servant to have rule over princes. Proverbs 19:10
2. He that turneth away his ear from hearing the law, even his prayer shall be abomination. Proverbs 28:9

I. Receives Stripes

1. Judgements are prepared for scorners, and stripes for the back of fools. Proverbs 19:29
2. A whip for the horse, a bridle for the ass, and a rod for the fool's back. Proverbs 26:3
3. Though thou shouldest bray a fool in a

mortar among wheat with a pestle, yet will not his foolishness depart from him. Proverbs 27:22

J. Calls for Strokes

A fool's lips enter into contention, and his mouth calleth for strokes. Proverbs 18:6

K. Receives No Honour

As snow in summer, and as rain in harvest, so honour is not seemly for a fool. Proverbs 26:1

IV. Warnings Against the Foolish Man

A. Forsake Him

Forsake the foolish, and live; and go in the way of understanding. Proverbs 9:6

B. Go from His Presence

Go from the presence of a foolish man, when thou perceivest not in him the lips of knowledge. Proverbs 14:7

C. Answer Him Not

Answer not a fool according to his folly, lest thou also be like unto him. Proverbs 26:4

D. Answer Him

Answer a fool according to his folly, lest he be wise in his own conceit. Proverbs 26:5

Chapter 2

THE SCORNFUL MAN

Proverbs 29:8
Scornful men bring a city into a
snare: but wise men turn
away wrath.

The reaction of the Wise Man is directly opposite of the Scornful Man. The Scornful Man is known as an extreme critic. He is not happy with what anyone is doing and does not hesitate to let those around him know about it. A scornful person shows his spirit by his words and the attitude in his actions. The Scornful Man dwells on the negative and not on the positive. If he is in the position of leadership, he will lead in the wrong direction. A scorner should be corrected so that the Simple Man, who may be following him, will take note (Proverbs 19:25). The Scornful Man delights in bringing reproach upon authority because he dislikes being corrected.

Most people do not care for scorners. They are poor company, and even a lost man does not want to spend time with a person who is negative all the time. Since the scornful man is not wise enough to accept reproof or instruction, he can only get worse.

It is possible for a saved person to be a scorner, but it shows that he does not walk with the Lord.

The Scornful Man

Dictionary "SCORNER": One who holds extreme contempt; to despise, to condemn.

Hebrew "SCORNER": To make mouths at; to scoff or mock; have in derision (3887); derision, scorning (3944).

I. Actions of the Scornful Man
A. Causes Contention, Strife, and Reproach

Job's Friends
Job 19:1-3

> Cast out the scorner, and contention shall go out; yea, strife and reproach shall cease.
> Proverbs 22:10

B. Speaks Against Corrective Authority

Korah
Numbers 16:1-3

1. He that reproveth a scorner getteth to himself shame: and he that rebuketh a wicked man getteth himself a blot. Proverbs 9:7
2. Reprove not a scorner, lest he hate thee: rebuke a wise man, and he will love thee. Proverbs 9:8
3. An ungodly witness scorneth judgment: and the mouth of the wicked devoureth iniquity. Proverbs 19:28

C. Delights in His Scorning

Pharisees
Mark 12:13-17

> How long, ye simple ones, will ye love

22

simplicity? and the scorners delight in their scorning, and fools hate knowledge? Proverbs 1:22

D. Hurts Others

Nebuchadnezzar
Daniel 3:19-22

Scornful men bring a city into a snare: but wise men turn away wrath. Proverbs 29:8

II. Characteristics of the Scornful Man
A. Will Not Listen to Correction

Hophni and
Phinehas
I Samuel 2:22-25

1. Reprove not a scorner, lest he hate thee: rebuke a wise man, and he will love thee. Proverbs 9:8
2. A wise son heareth his father's instruction: but a scorner heareth not rebuke. Proverbs 13:1
3. A scorner loveth not one that reproveth him: neither will he go unto the wise. Proverbs 15:12

B. Will Not Find Wisdom

Rehoboam
I Kings 12:6-13

A scorner seeketh wisdom, and findeth it not: but knowledge is easy unto him that understandeth. Proverbs 14:6

III. Consequences of the Scornful Man
A. Is Full of Wrath, Due to Pride
1. Proud and haughty scorner is his name, who dealeth in proud wrath. Proverbs 21:24

23

2. Scornful men bring a city into a snare: but wise men turn away wrath. Proverbs 29:8

B. Is Corrected by God

Surely he scorneth the scorners: but he giveth grace unto the lowly. Proverbs 3:34

C. Is an Abomination to Men

The thought of foolishness is sin: and the scorner is an abomination to men. Proverbs 24:9

Chapter 3

THE WISE MAN

Proverbs 9:9
Give instruction to a wise man, and
he will be yet wiser: teach a just man,
and he will increase in learning.

The Wise Man is the main topic in the book of Proverbs. Even the verses that do not specifically mention the Wise Man illustrate ways that men are, or are not, like him.

Proverbs gives sixteen different actions of the Wise Man. The key to all of them is in Proverbs 9:10, "The fear of the Lord . . ." By fearing God, most of the other actions will come naturally. A man who fears God will be a soul winner, accept correction, and depart from evil.

According to Proverbs 3, wisdom is better than gold, silver, rubies, and all the things you can desire. Hence, a Wise Man is extremely valuable.

One of the most outstanding attributes of a Wise Man is that he is willing to accept reproof and instruction. Many people want wisdom, but they don't like the package it comes in. They are not willing to accept reproof, which is the carrying case for wisdom. Consequently, the man who thinks he is rejecting reproof is in reality, rejecting wisdom.

Oh, if all Christians would strive to be wise; their actions would be enjoyable, their characteristics would be favorable, and their end would be glorious.

The Wise Man

Dictionary "WISE": Properly having knowledge: hence having the power of discerning and judging correctly, or of discriminating between what is true and what is false. The discreet use or application of knowledge.

Hebrew "WISE": To be wise in mind, word, or act (2499).
Note: Knowledge + Understanding = Wisdom (Proverbs 2:6).

I. Actions of the Wise Man
A. Listens

Samuel
I Samuel 3:10

> A wise man will hear, and will increase learning; and a man of understanding shall attain unto wise counsels. Proverbs 1:5

B. Accepts Correction

David
II Samuel 12:7-13
Psalm 51:3

1. Reprove not a scorner, lest he hate thee: rebuke a wise man, and he will love thee. Proverbs 9:8
2. Give instruction to a wise man, and he will be yet wiser: teach a just man, and he will increase in learning. Proverbs 9:9
3. The ear that heareth the reproof of life abideth among the wise. Proverbs 15:31
4. A reproof entereth more into a wise man than an hundred stripes into a fool. Proverbs 17:10
5. The rod and reproof give wisdom: but a child left to himself bringeth his mother to shame. Proverbs 29:15

C. Prepares

Ezra
Ezra 7:10

He that gathereth in summer is a wise son: but he that sleepeth in harvest is a son that causeth shame. Proverbs 10:5

D. Follows Instruction

Jehoash
II Kings 12:2

1. The wise in heart will receive commandments: but a prating fool shall fall. Proverbs 10:8
2. A wise son heareth his father's instruction: but a scorner heareth not rebuke. Proverbs 13:1
3. Hear counsel, and receive instruction, that thou mayest be wise in thy latter end. Proverbs 19:20

E. Gains Knowledge

Timothy
II Timothy 3:14,15

1. Wise men lay up knowledge: but the mouth of the foolish is near destruction. Proverbs 10:14
2. The tongue of the wise useth knowledge aright: but the mouth of fools poureth out foolishness. Proverbs 15:2
3. The lips of the wise disperse knowledge: but the heart of the foolish doeth not so. Proverbs 15:7
4. The heart of the wise teacheth his mouth, and addeth learning to his lips. Proverbs 16:23
5. The heart of the prudent getteth knowledge; and the ear of the wise seeketh knowledge. Proverbs 18:15
6. When the scorner is punished, the simple is made

wise: and when the wise is instructed, he receiveth knowledge. Proverbs 21:11

F.   Refrains His Tongue

Jesus
  John 8:4-9

1. In the multitude of words there wanteth not sin: but he that refraineth his lips is wise. Proverbs 10:19
2. Even a fool, when he holdeth his peace, is counted wise: and he that shutteth his lips is esteemed a man of understanding. Proverbs 17:28
3. A fool uttereth all his mind: but a wise man keepeth it in till afterwards. Proverbs 29:11

G.   Wins Souls

Peter &
Apostles
  Acts 5:40-42

The fruit of the righteous is a tree of life; and he that winneth souls is wise. Proverbs 11:30

H.   Hearkens to Counsel

Apollos
  Acts 18:24-28

1. The way of a fool is right in his own eyes: but he that hearkeneth unto counsel is wise. Proverbs 12:15
2. Only by pride cometh contention: but with the well advised is wisdom. Proverbs 13:10
3. Hear counsel, and receive instruction, that thou mayest be wise in thy latter end. Proverbs 19:20

I. Walks with Wise Men

Elisha
II Kings 2:1-11

He that walketh with wise men shall be wise: but a companion of fools shall be destroyed. Proverbs 13:20

J. Departs from Evil

Joseph
Genesis 39:9, 10

A wise man feareth, and departeth from evil: but the fool rageth, and is confident. Proverbs 14:16

K. Abstains from Liquor

Daniel
Daniel 1:8

Wine is a mocker, strong drink is raging: and whosoever is deceived thereby is not wise. Proverbs 20:1

L. Obeys God's Law

Josiah
II Kings 23:1-25

Whoso keepeth the law is a wise son: but he that is a companion of riotous men shameth his father. Proverbs 28:7

M. Gets Understanding

Bezaleel
Exodus 35:30-33

1. Counsel is mine, and sound wisdom: I am understanding; I have strength. Proverbs 8:14
2. In the lips of him that hath understanding wisdom is found: but a rod is for the back of him that is void of understanding. Proverbs 10:13
3. It is as sport to a fool to do mischief: but a man of understanding hath wisdom. Proverbs 10:23
4. Wisdom resteth in the heart of him that hath understanding: but that which is in the midst of fools is made known. Proverbs 14:33
5. Wisdom is before him that hath understanding; but the eyes of a fool are in the ends of the earth. Proverbs 17:24

N. Fears God

Job
Job 1:1, 8; 2:3

1. The fear of the LORD is the beginning of wisdom: and the knowledge of the holy is understanding. Proverbs 9:10
2. The fear of the LORD is a fountain of life, to depart from the snares of death. Proverbs 14:27
3. The fear of the LORD is the instruction of wisdom; and before honor is humility. Proverbs 15:33

O. Shows Respect for Others

Good Samaritan
Luke 10:30-37

He that is void of wisdom despiseth his neighbour: but a man of understanding holdeth his peace. Proverbs 11:12

P.   Knows Prudence

Solomon
II Chronicles 2:11,12

1. I wisdom dwell with prudence, and find out knowledge of witty inventions. Proverbs 8:12
2. The wisdom of the prudent is to understand his way: but the folly of fools is deceit. Proverbs 14:8
3. The wise in heart shall be called prudent: and the sweetness of the lips increaseth learning. Proverbs 16:21

II.   Characteristics of the Wise Man
A.   Is Fair and Just

Moses
Numbers 27:1-11

1. The mouth of the just bringeth forth wisdom: but the froward tongue shall be cut out. Proverbs 10:31
2. These things also belong to the wise. It is not good to have respect of persons in judgement. Proverbs 24:23

B.   Is Patient

Paul
II Corinthians 12:7-11

Scornful men bring a city into a snare: but wise men turn away wrath. Proverbs 29:8

C. Is Humble

The Centurion
Matthew 8:5-8

When pride cometh, then cometh shame: but with the lowly is wisdom. Proverbs 11:2

III. Rewards of the Wise Man

A. Receives Honour

1. Length of days is in her right hand; and in her left hand riches and honour. Proverbs 3:16
2. The wise shall inherit glory: but shame shall be the promotion of fools. Proverbs 3:35
3. Exalt her, and she shall promote thee: she shall bring thee to honour, when thou dost embrace her. Proverbs 4:8
4. She shall give to thine head an ornament of grace: a crown of glory shall she deliver to thee. Proverbs 4:9
5. A man shall be commended according to his wisdom: but he that is of a perverse heart shall be despised. Proverbs 12:8

B. Has a Glad Father

1. The proverbs of Solomon. A wise son maketh a glad father: but a foolish son is the heaviness of his mother. Proverbs 10:1
2. A wise son maketh a glad father: but a foolish man despiseth his mother. Proverbs 15:20
3. My son, if thine heart be wise, my heart shall rejoice, even mine. Proverbs 23:15
4. The father of the righteous shall greatly rejoice: and he that begetteth a wise child shall have joy of him. Proverbs 23:24
5. My son, be wise, and make my heart glad, that I may answer him that reproacheth me. Proverbs 27:11
6. Whoso loveth wisdom rejoiceth his father: but he that keepeth company with harlots spendeth his substance. Proverbs 29:3

C. Obtains Favour
1. For whoso findeth me findeth life, and shall obtain favour of the LORD. Proverbs 8:35
2. The king's favour is toward a wise servant: but his wrath is against him that causeth shame. Proverbs 14:35
3. He that handleth a matter wisely shall find good: and whoso trusteth in the LORD, happy is he. Proverbs 16:20

D. Has Length of Days
Length of days is in her right hand; and in her left hand riches and honour. Proverbs 3:16

E. Possesses Riches
Length of days is in her right hand; and in her left hand riches and honour. Proverbs 3:16

F. Has Ways of Pleasantness
Her ways are ways of pleasantness, and all her paths are peace. Proverbs 3:17

G. Receives Peace
Her ways are ways of pleasantness, and all her paths are peace. Proverbs 3:17

H. Has Happiness
1. Happy is the man that findeth wisdom, and the man that getteth understanding. Proverbs 3:13
2. She is a tree of life to them that lay hold upon her: and happy is every one that retaineth her. Proverbs 3:18

I. Is Protected
Forsake her not, and she shall preserve thee: love her, and she shall keep thee. Proverbs 4:6

J. Is Rewarded
So shall the knowledge of wisdom be unto thy soul: when thou hast found it, then there shall be a reward, and thy expectation shall not be cut off. Proverbs 24:14

K. Is Delivered
He that trusteth in his own heart is a fool: but whoso walketh wisely, he shall be delivered. Proverbs 28:26

Chapter 4

THE SIMPLE MAN

Proverbs 9:4, 5
Whoso is simple, let him turn in
hither: as for him that wanteth
understanding, she saith to him, Come,
eat of my bread, and drink of the
wine which I have mingled.

In the Bible, the Prudent Man's opposite is the Simple Man. Approximately eighty percent of an average audience is made up of Simple Men. Whether it be a classroom or a church congregation, the majority of the people will be simple.

The Simple Man has the distinct characteristic of being easily allured or deceived. The Simple Man feels extremely comfortable in a crowd, since so many of those around him are just like him. In a classroom situation, the twenty percent who are not considered Simple Men are usually made up of equal parts of Wise and Scornful Men.

The Simple Man is a constant concern to his pastor. The pastor must continually strive to get the church member grounded in God's Word so that he is not moved about by every wind of doctrine.

The natural state of every man is to be simple. The Christian should, with God's help, strive to overcome this weakness and be prudent.

The Simple Man

Dictionary "SIMPLE": Weak in intellect; not wise or sagacious; silly.

Hebrew "SIMPLE": Silly; seducible (6612) to open; make roomy: delude; allure; deceive; enlarge; entice; persuade (6601). Note: Adding "able" on the end of each word describes the simple man.

I. Actions of the Simple Man
A. Believes Every Word

Amasa
II Samuel 20:9, 10

> The simple believeth every word: but the prudent man looketh well to his going. Proverbs 14:15

B. Learns from the Punishment of the Scorner

Israelites
Deuteronomy 17:12,13

> 1. Smite a scorner, and the simple will beware: and reprove one that hath understanding, and he will understand knowledge. Proverbs 19:25
> 2. When the scorner is punished, the simple is made wise: and when the wise is instructed, he receiveth knowledge. Proverbs 21:11

C. Does Evil

Samson
Judges 16:1-31

> A prudent man foreseeth the evil, and hideth himself: but the simple pass on, and are punished. Proverbs 22:3; 27:12

II. Characteristic of the Simple Man
Is without Understanding

A Man of God
I Kings 13:7-24

> And beheld among the simple ones, I discerned among the youths, a young man void of understanding, Proverbs 7:7

III. Consequences of the Simple Man
A. Inherits Folly

> The simple inherit folly: but the prudent are crowned with knowledge. Proverbs 14:18

B. Does Evil and Is Punished

> A prudent man foreseeth the evil, and hideth himself: but the simple pass on, and are punished. Proverbs 22:3; 27:12

39

Chapter 5

THE PRUDENT MAN

Proverbs 27:12
A prudent man foreseeth the evil, and
hideth himself; but the simple pass on,
and are punished.

The Prudent Man is the opposite of the Simple Man. The most prevalent quality of the Prudent Man is his foresight. His mind is not so caught up with the present that he does not give thought to the future. He is noted for his carefulness and his ability to be observant in everyday life situations. He is constantly learning. He fully realizes that the knowledge gained at present, though not immediately necessary, may prove to be valuable in the future. He will contemplate the reproof he receives to see what adjustments should be made to prevent the same thing from happening again. Being able to foresee problems and avoid problems are characteristics all Christians need.

The Prudent Man

Dictionary "PRUDENT":   Cautious; circumspect; careful of the consequences; measures or actions.

Hebrew "PRUDENT":   Cunning (6175); to separate mentally, distinguish; beware; intelligent; guide wittingly; crafty; subtil (995).

I.   Actions of the Prudent Man

A.   Controls Temper

Jesus
Matthew 27:12-14

A fool's wrath is presently known: but a prudent man covereth shame. Proverbs 12:16

B.   Conceals Knowledge

Jehu
II Kings 10:18-25

A prudent man concealeth knowledge: but the heart of fools proclaimeth foolishness. Proverbs 12:23

C.   Gathers Knowledge

Paul
II Timothy 4:13

1. Every prudent man dealeth with knowledge: but a fool layeth open his folly. Proverbs 13:16
2. The simple inherit folly: but the prudent are crowned with knowledge. Proverbs 14:18
3. The heart of the prudent getteth knowledge; and the ear of the wise seeketh knowledge. Proverbs 18:15

D. Heeds Reproof

David
II Samuel 12:7-14

> A fool despiseth his father's instruction: but he that regardeth reproof is prudent. Proverbs 15:5

E. Forsees Sin

Joseph
Genesis 39:7-10

> A prudent man foreseeth the evil, and hideth himself: but the simple pass on, and are punished. Proverbs 22:3; 27:12
> Dictionary "FORSEETH": to see, advise self; consider.
> Dictionary "HIDETH": to hide; be absent; conceal.

II. Characteristics of the Prudent Man
A. Understands His Way

Hananiah, Mishael, & Azariah
Daniel 3:16-18

> 1. The wisdom of the prudent is to understand his way: but the folly of fools is deceit. Proverbs 14:8
> 2. The simple believeth every word: but the prudent man looketh well to his going. Proverbs 14:15

B. Has Wisdom

Solomon
II Chronicles 2:12

> 1. I wisdom dwell with prudence, and find out knowledge of witty inventions. Proverbs 8:12
> 2. The wise in heart shall be called prudent: and the sweetness of the lips increaseth learning. Proverbs 16:21

Chapter 6

THE SLOTHFUL MAN

Proverbs 22:13
The slothful man saith, There is a lion
without, I shall be slain in the streets.

The Diligent Man's opposite is the Slothful Man. He is lazy, idle, indolent, and is often referred to as a sluggard. He has a distinct distaste for work. Though he often has the ability to accomplish a given task, he lacks the initiative needed to carry it through. He tries to find an excuse for not doing his work. Proverbs lists two of his excuses as the "cold" weather and a "lion" in the way.

There are slothful men everywhere. On the job, they force others to take up the slack caused by their own laziness.

Another interesting characteristic of the Slothful Man is his wastefulness. Cars, possessions, and even food are always appreciated more when a person has had to work for them. Many of today's generation are wasteful because they have been given too much. They have no sense of responsibility, consequently, they feel that the world owes them!

The Slothful Man's characteristics make him unpleasant company. Christians who are slothful are a very bad testimony for their Saviour.

The Slothful Man

Dictionary "SLOTHFUL": Inactive; sluggish; lazy; idle.

Hebrew "SLOTHFUL": Indolent, slothful; sluggard (6102); to lean idly (6101).

I. Actions of the Slothful Man
A. Makes Excuses

Slothful Servant
Matthew 25:24-28

1. The sluggard will not plow by reason of the cold; therefore shall he beg in harvest, and have nothing. Proverbs 20:4
2. The slothful man saith, There is a lion without, I shall be slain in the streets. Proverbs 22:13
3. The slothful man saith, There is a lion in the way; a lion is in the streets. Proverbs 26:13
4. The sluggard is wiser in his own conceit than seven men that can render a reason. Proverbs 26:16

B. Sleeps

Disciples
Matthew 26:36-46

1. How long wilt thou sleep, O sluggard? when wilt thou arise out of thy sleep? Yet a little sleep, a little slumber, a little folding of the hands to sleep: Proverbs 6:9,10
2. Slothfulness casteth into a deep sleep; and an idle soul shall suffer hunger. Proverbs 19:15
3. As the door turneth upon his hinges, so doth the slothful upon his bed. Proverbs 26:14

II. Characteristics of the Slothful Man
A. Is Wasteful

Unjust Steward
Luke 16:1-4

1. The slothful man roasteth not that which he took in hunting: but the substance of a diligent man is precious. Proverbs 12:27
2. He also that is slothful in his work is brother to him that is a great waster. Proverbs 18:9

B. Is Lazy

Ahab
I Kings 21:1-4

1. A slothful man hideth his hand in his bosom, and will not so much as bring it to his mouth again. Proverbs 19:24
2. The slothful hideth his hand in his bosom; it grieveth him to bring it again to his mouth. Proverbs 26:15

C. Refuses to Work

Some at Thessalonica
II Thessalonians 3:8-12

1. The desire of the slothful killeth him; for his hands refuse to labour. Proverbs 21:25
2. I went by the field of the slothful, and by the vineyard of the man void of understanding; And, lo, it was all grown over with thorns, and nettles had covered the face thereof, and the stone wall thereof was broken down. Proverbs 24:30,31

III. Consequences of the Slothful Man

A. Is Burdened

The hand of the diligent shall bear rule: but the slothful shall be under tribute. Proverbs 12:24

Dictionary "TRIBUTE": a burden

B. Has Problems and Trouble

The way of the slothful man is as an hedge of thorns: but the way of the righteous is made plain. Proverbs 15:19

C. Becomes Poor

1. The soul of the sluggard desireth, and hath nothing: but the soul of the diligent shall be made fat. Proverbs 13:4

2. The sluggard will not plow by reason of the cold; therefore shall he beg in harvest, and have nothing. Proverbs 20:4

3. I went by the field of the slothful, and by the vineyard of the man void of understanding; Proverbs 24:30

4. So shall thy poverty come as one that travelleth; and thy want as an armed man. Proverbs 24:34

Chapter 7

THE DILIGENT MAN

Proverbs 22:29
Seest thou a man diligent in his busi-
ness? he shall stand before kings; he
shall not stand before mean men.

In every respect, the Diligent Man is the opposite of the Slothful Man. His work is marked by his unswerving determination and his enthusiasm and zeal to get something done. He is dependable and can be trusted to finish his tasks. He is not half-hearted in his efforts. He believes that a job worth doing is worth doing right. He never considers quitting a job before it is finished, or procrastinating until a later date.

The Diligent Man is often given a responsibility such as an overseer or foreman. Because of his characteristics, the Diligent Man is a favorite at any work place. He will also be rewarded for his diligence, as God promises in Galatians 6:7, ". . . Whatsoever a man soweth, that shall he also reap."

The Diligent Man

Dictionary "DILIGENT": Constant in effort or exertion to accomplish what is undertaken; industrious.

Hebrew "DILIGENT": Incised, incisive; determination, eager-decision; to point sharply (2742).

I. Actions of the Diligent Man
A. Works Hard

Epaphroditus
Philippians 2:25-30

> He becometh poor that dealeth with a slack hand: but the hand of the diligent maketh rich.
> Proverbs 10:4
> Dictionary "SLACK": remissness, idle, slothful

B. Is Prepared

David
I Chron. 22:5, 14;
29:2-3

1. Seest thou a man diligent in his business? he shall stand before kings; he shall not stand before mean men. Proverbs 22:29
2. Be thou diligent to know the state of thy flocks, and look well to thy herds. Proverbs 27:23

II. Characteristics of the Diligent Man
A. Is Not Wasteful

Jesus
John 6:1-13

The slothful man roasteth not that which he took

in hunting: but the substance of a diligent man is precious. Proverbs 12:27

B.   Plans

Joseph
Genesis 41:32-40

The thoughts of the diligent tend only to plenteousness; but of everyone that is hasty only to want. Proverbs 21:5

III. Rewards of the Diligent Man
A.   Has Riches
He becometh poor that dealeth with a slack hand: but the hand of the diligent maketh rich.
Proverbs 10:4
B.   Is in a Place of Authority
The hand of the diligent shall bear rule: but the slothful shall be under tribute. Proverbs 12:24
C.   Is Satisfied
The soul of the sluggard desireth, and hath nothing: but the soul of the diligent shall be made fat. Proverbs 13:4
Dictionary "SOUL": breathing creature.
Dictionary "FAT": to be fat (figurative) to satisfy.
D.   Has Plenty
The thoughts of the diligent tend only to plenteousness; but of every one that is hasty only to want. Proverbs 21:5

Chapter 8

THE POOR MAN

Proverbs 28:3
A poor man that oppresseth the poor
is like a sweeping rain which
leaveth no food.

The opposite of the Rich Man is, of course, the Poor Man. He does without many things because he has no alternative. His income is considerably less than adequate; consequently, he dresses, eats, and acts differently than those who have sufficient income.

In today's society, many people who are poor have chosen to be poor. The book of Proverbs shows eight ways that a man becomes poor. All eight ways are due to a lack of character. The primary reason for poverty is laziness. Four different times Proverbs refers to poverty as a result of slothfulness.

Being poor is not a sin itself, although, it is often caused by sin. By living within his means, the poor man can be godly.

Unfortunately, most people do not care about the Poor Man. Yet, God warns Christians to give to the poor. Christians are also warned not to oppress or mock the poor. God loves all men whether they are rich or poor.

The Christian who is poor should try to get out of debt by giving God His part and trusting Him to make ends meet.

The Poor Man

Dictionary "POOR": Wholly destitute of property, or not having property sufficient for a comfortable substance.

Hebrew "POOR": To be destitute; lack; needy (7326); deficiency, lack, penury, poverty (4270).

I. Actions of the Poor Man
A. Does Not Hear Rebuke

Mordecai
Esther 3:2-5

The ransom of a man's life are his riches: but the poor heareth not rebuke. Proverbs 13:8

B. Refuses Instruction

Prodigal Son
Luke 15:12-19

Poverty and shame shall be to him that refuseth instruction: but he that regardeth reproof shall be honoured. Proverbs 13:18

C. Does Not Expect Help

Bartimaeus
Mark 10:46-52

The poor useth intreaties; but the rich answereth roughly. Proverbs 18:23
Dictionary "ENTREATIES": earnest prayer, supplications.

II. Consequences of the Poor Man
A. Is Hated by His Neighbor
1. The poor is hated even of his own neighbour: but the rich hath many friends. Proverbs 14:20
2. Wealth maketh many friends; but the poor is separated from his neighbour. Proverbs 19:4

B. Is Hated by His Brethren
All the brethren of the poor do hate him: how much more do his friends go far from him? he pursueth them with words, yet they are wanting to him. Proverbs 19:7

C. Is Forsaken by His Friends
All the brethren of the poor do hate him: how much more do his friends go far from him? he pursueth them with words, yet they are wanting to him. Proverbs 19:7

D. Is Rebuked by the Rich
The rich ruleth over the poor, and the borrower is servant to the lender. Proverbs 22:7

III. Ways to Become a Poor Man
A. Be Slothful
1. How long wilt thou sleep, O sluggard? when wilt thou arise out of thy sleep? Yet a little sleep, a little slumber, a little folding of the hands to sleep: So shall thy poverty come as one that travelleth, and thy want as an armed man. Proverbs 6:9-11
2. He becometh poor that dealeth with a slack hand: but the hand of the diligent maketh rich. Proverbs 10:4
   Hebrew "SLACK": remissness, idle, slothful (7423).
3. I went by the field of the slothful, and by the vineyard of the man void of understanding; So shall thy poverty come as one that travelleth; and thy want as an armed man. Proverbs 24:30, 34

B. Be Selfish and Greedy
There is that scattereth, and yet increaseth; and

there is that withholdeth more than is meet, but it tendeth to poverty. Proverbs 11:24

C. Lack Judgment

Much food is in the tillage of the poor: but there is that is destroyed for want of judgment. Proverbs 13:23

D. Love Sleep

1. Love not sleep, lest thou come to poverty; open thine eyes, and thou shalt be satisfied with bread. Proverbs 20:13

2. For the drunkard and the glutton shall come to poverty: and drowsiness shall clothe a man with rags. Proverbs 23:21

E. Love Pleasure

He that loveth pleasure shall be a poor man: he that loveth wine and oil shall not be rich. Proverbs 21:17

F. Oppress the Poor or Give to the Rich

1. He that oppresseth the poor to increase his riches, and he that giveth to the rich, shall surely come to want. Proverbs 22:16

2. A poor man that oppresseth the poor is like a sweeping rain which leaveth no food. Proverbs 28:3

G. Be a Drunkard

For the drunkard and the glutton shall come to poverty: and drowsiness shall clothe a man with rags. Proverbs 23:21

H. Be a Glutton

For the drunkard and the glutton shall come to poverty: and drowsiness shall clothe a man with rags. Proverbs 23:21

IV. Warnings in Favor of the Poor Man

A. Give to the Poor

1. He that despiseth his neighbour sinneth: but he that hath mercy on the poor, happy is he. Proverbs 14:21

2. He that hath pity upon the poor lendeth unto the LORD; and that which he hath given will he pay him again. Proverbs 19:17

3. He that giveth unto the poor shall not lack: but he that hideth his eyes shall have many a curse. Proverbs 28:27

B. Do Not Oppress the Poor

He that oppresseth the poor reproacheth his Maker: but he that honoureth him hath mercy on the poor. Proverbs 14:31

C. Do Not Mock the Poor

Whoso mocketh the poor reproacheth his Maker: and he that is glad at calamities shall not be unpunished. Proverbs 17:5

D. Do Not Ignore the Poor

Whoso stoppeth his ears at the cry of the poor, he also shall cry himself, but shall not be heard. Proverbs 21:13

E. Do Not Rob the Poor

Rob not the poor, because he is poor: neither oppress the afflicted in the gate: For the LORD will plead their cause, and spoil the soul of those that spoiled them. Proverbs 22:22, 23

Dictionary "SPOIL": To cover, defraud; rob.

V. A Poor Man is Better Than…

A. A Fool if He Has Integrity

Better is the poor that walketh in his integrity, than he that is perverse in his lips, and is a fool. Proverbs 19:1

B. A Liar

The desire of a man is his kindness: and a poor man is better than a liar. Proverbs 19:22

C. A Rich Man Who Is Perverse in His Ways

Better is the poor that walketh in his uprightness, than he that is perverse in his ways, though he be rich. Proverbs 28:6

Chapter 9

THE RICH MAN

Proverbs 28:11
The rich man is wise in his own
conceit; but the poor that hath
understanding searcheth him out.

Opposite of the Poor Man is the Rich Man. Although the Bible does not condemn those who are rich, it warns them to be careful. Money often changes people's attitudes and actions. Becoming rich should not be the ultimate goal of a Christian. In Proverbs 23:4, God warns, "Labour not to be rich . . ." The Christian's primary purpose for making money should be to sustain his family and to further the cause of Christ. Many have forgotten this cause and "laboured" to build up a bank account. A Christian should not labor to be rich, but if he is rich, then God has instructions for him to follow. Riches obtained and utilized in the proper manner can be a blessing. Proverbs lists several positive ways to become rich. These do not include perverse actions such as stealing, cheating, or lying.

God's desire is to see Christians prosper! Proverbs 10:22 says, "The blessing of the LORD, it maketh rich . . . " It is not wrong to be rich, it is only wrong to want to be rich. It is not how much you have, but what you do with what you have that counts.

The Rich Man

Dictionary "RICH": Wealthy; possessing a large portion of lands, ground, or money.

Hebrew "RICH": Rich (6223); to accumulate, to grow rich (6238).

I.   Actions of the Rich Man
A.   Answers Roughly

Nabal
  I Samuel 25:1-11

> The poor useth intreaties; but the rich answereth roughly. Proverbs 18:23

B.   Rules over the Poor

Pharaoh
  Exodus 1:8-11

> The rich ruleth over the poor, and the borrower is servant to the lender. Proverbs 22:7

C.   Is Wise in His Own Conceit

Haman
  Esther 5:9-11

> The rich man is wise in his own conceit; but the poor that hath understanding searcheth him out. Proverbs 28:11

II.   Characteristic of the Rich Man
He Has Friends

Jehoshaphat
  II Chronicles 18:1,2

1. The poor is hated even of his own neighbour: but the rich hath many friends. Proverbs 14:20
2. Wealth maketh many friends; but the poor is separated from his neighbour. Proverbs 19:4
3. Many will intreat the favour of the prince: and every man is a friend to him that giveth gifts. Proverbs 19:6

III. How to be Rich
A. Get Wisdom
1. Length of days is in her right hand; and in her left hand riches and honour. Proverbs 3:16
2. Riches and honour are with me; yea, durable riches and righteousness. Proverbs 8:18
3. The crown of the wise is their riches: but the foolishness of fools is folly. Proverbs 14:24
4. Through wisdom is an house builded; and by understanding it is established: And by knowledge shall the chambers be filled with all precious and pleasant riches. Proverbs 24:3,4

B. Be Diligent
He becometh poor that dealeth with a slack hand: but the hand of the diligent maketh rich. Proverbs 10:4

C. Have the Blessing of the Lord
The blessing of the LORD, it maketh rich, and he addeth no sorrow with it. Proverbs 10:22

D. Work
Wealth gotten by vanity shall be diminished: but he that gathereth by labour shall increase. Proverbs 13:11

E. Receive an Inheritance
House and riches are the inheritance of fathers: and a prudent wife is from the LORD. Proverbs 19:14

F. Be Humble and Fear God
By humility and the fear of the LORD are riches, and honour, and life. Proverbs 22:4

IV. Warnings Concerning Riches

A. Do Not Trust in Riches or You Will Fall

He that trusteth in his riches shall fall: but the righteous shall flourish as a branch. Proverbs 11:28

B. Do Not Oppress the Poor to Increase Your Riches

He that oppresseth the poor to increase his riches, and he that giveth to the rich, shall surely come to want. Proverbs 22:16

C. Do Not Give to the Rich

He that oppresseth the poor to increase his riches, and he that giveth to the rich, shall surely come to want. Proverbs 22:16

D. Do Not Labor to Be Rich

1. Labour not to be rich: cease from thine own wisdom. Proverbs 23:4
2. Wilt thou set thine eyes upon that which is not? for riches certainly make themselves wings; they fly away as an eagle toward heaven. Proverbs 23:5

E. Do Not Make Haste to Be Rich

1. A faithful man shall abound with blessings: but he that maketh haste to be rich shall not be innocent. Proverbs 28:20
2. He that hasteth to be rich hath an evil eye, and considereth not that poverty shall come upon him. Proverbs 28:22

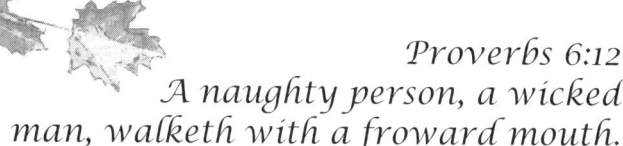

Chapter 10

THE WICKED MAN

Proverbs 6:12
A naughty person, a wicked
man, walketh with a froward mouth.

The Wicked Man is the contrast of the Righteous Man. Throughout the book of Proverbs, the Wicked Man represents the lost man. One verse Proverbs 21:12 says, ". . . God overthroweth the wicked for their wickedness." Another verse, Proverbs 15:29, says, "The LORD is far from the wicked: . . . " Proverbs 12:2 states, ". . . a man of wicked devices will he condemn." The entire book points to the fact that the Wicked Man is a lost man.

Most of the verses that talk about the Wicked Man portray him as a contrast of the Righteous Man. The verses show the difference between the lost and the saved.

Any Christian who works with a lost man can actually see that man's characteristics listed in the book of Proverbs. The Wicked Man has no feelings for the Christian and will often do all he can to destroy the Christian's testimony. ". . . for what fellowship hath righteousness with unrighteousness? . . . " II Corinthians 6:14

The solution for the Wicked Man is, of course, salvation. Perhaps through the testimony of a Christian, the Wicked Man will see his need for salvation and receive Christ. Only by putting his trust in a righteous God can the wicked man become righteous.

The Wicked Man

Dictionary "WICKED": Evil in principle or practice; deviating from the divine law; addicted to vice; sinful, immoral.

Hebrew "WICKED": Morally wrong; an actively bad person (7563); guilty, ungodly.

I.   Actions of the Wicked Man
A.   Speaks Frowardly

Goliath
I Samuel 17:43

1.   A naughty person, a wicked man, walketh with a froward mouth. Proverbs 6:12
2.   The lips of the righteous know what is acceptable: but the mouth of the wicked speaketh frowardness. Proverbs 10:32
3.   The heart of the righteous studieth to answer: but the mouth of the wicked poureth out evil things. Proverbs 15:28

B.   Criticizes Authority When Rebuked

Korah
Numbers 16:1-33

He that reproveth a scorner getteth to himself shame: and he that rebuketh a wicked man getteth himself a blot. Proverbs 9:7

C.   Speaks with Cruelty and Damage

Saul
Acts 9:1

1.   Blessings are upon the head of the just: but

68

violence covereth the mouth of the wicked. Proverbs 10:6

2. The mouth of a righteous man is a well of life: but violence covereth the mouth of the wicked. Proverbs 10:11

3. By the blessing of the upright the city is exalted: but it is overthrown by the mouth of the wicked. Proverbs 11:11

4. The words of the wicked are to lie in wait for blood: but the mouth of the upright shall deliver them. Proverbs 12:6

5. When the righteous are in authority, the people rejoice: but when the wicked beareth rule, the people mourn. Proverbs 29:2

D. Seduces the Righteous

Absalom
II Samuel 15:1-6

The righteous is more excellent than his neighbour: but the way of the wicked seduceth them. Proverbs 12:26

E. Lies

Ananias
Acts 5:1-6

1. A righteous man hateth lying: but a wicked man is loathsome, and cometh to shame. Proverbs 13:5

2. If a ruler hearken to lies, all his servants are wicked. Proverbs 29:12

F. Listens to Gossip

Artaxerxes
Ezra 4:11-24

69

A wicked doer giveth heed to false lips; and a liar giveth ear to a naughty tongue. Proverbs 17:4

G. Bribes Authority

Balak
Numbers 22:1-7,
37-41

A wicked man taketh a gift out of the bosom to pervert the ways of judgment. Proverbs 17:23

H. Is Disrespectful

Shimei
II Samuel 16:5-8

When the wicked cometh, then cometh also contempt, and with ignominy reproach. Proverbs 18:3

I. Does Iniquity

Manasseh
II Kings 21:1-16

1. An ungodly witness scorneth judgment: and the mouth of the wicked devoureth iniquity. Proverbs 19:28
2. When the wicked are multiplied, transgression increaseth: but the righteous shall see their fall. Proverbs 29:16

J. Refuses to Condemn Sin

Ahab
I Kings 20:38-43

The robbery of the wicked shall destroy them; because they refuse to do judgment. Proverbs 21:7

K. Continues Stubbornly in Sin

Jeroboam
I Kings 12:28-33

> A wicked man hardeneth his face: but as for the upright, he directeth his way. Proverbs 21:29

II. Characteristics of the Wicked Man
A. Works a Deceitful Work

Judas
Luke 22:1-6

1. The righteous is delivered out of trouble, and the wicked cometh in his stead. Proverbs 11:8
2. The thoughts of the righteous are right: but the counsels of the wicked are deceit. Proverbs 12:5

B. Is Cruel to Animals

Balaam
Numbers 22:23-29

> A righteous man regardeth the life of his beast: but the tender mercies of the wicked are cruel. Proverbs 12:10

C. Desires Evil

Herod
Acts 12:1-4

1. The wicked desireth the net of evil men: but the root of the righteous yieldeth fruit. Proverbs 12:12
2. The soul of the wicked desireth evil: his neighbour findeth no favour in his eyes. Proverbs 21:10

71

D. Does Not Care about Poor People

A Levite
Luke 10:30-32

1. As a roaring lion, and a ranging bear; so is a wicked ruler over the poor people.
Proverbs 28:15
2. The righteous considereth the cause of the poor: but the wicked regardeth not to know it.
Proverbs 29:7

E. Does Not Like the Righteous

King of Egypt
Exodus 1:12-14

1. When righteous men do rejoice, there is great glory: but when the wicked rise, a man is hidden.
Proverbs 28:12
2. When the wicked rise, men hide themselves: but when they perish, the righteous increase.
Proverbs 28:28
3. An unjust man is an abomination to the just: and he that is upright in the way is abomination to the wicked. Proverbs 29:27

III. Consequences of the Wicked Man
A. Receives Destruction
1. But the wicked shall be cut off from the earth, and the transgressors shall be rooted out of it.
Proverbs 2:22
2. Be not afraid of sudden fear, neither of the desolation of the wicked, when it cometh.
Proverbs 3:25
3. As the whirlwind passeth, so is the wicked no more: but the righteous is an everlasting foundation. Proverbs 10:25
4. When it goeth well with the righteous, the city

rejoiceth: and when the wicked perish, there is shouting. Proverbs 11:10

5. Righteousness keepeth him that is upright in the way: but wickedness overthroweth the sinner. Proverbs 13:6

6. The heart knoweth his own bitterness; and a stranger doth not intermeddle with his joy. Proverbs 14:10

7. The robbery of the wicked shall destroy them; because they refuse to do judgment. Proverbs 21:7

B. Is Cursed of the Lord

The curse of the LORD is in the house of the wicked: but he blesseth the habitation of the just. Proverbs 3:33

C. Has Problems and Trouble

1. The way of the wicked is as darkness: they know not at what they stumble. Proverbs 4:19

2. The righteous is delivered out of trouble, and the wicked cometh in his stead. Proverbs 11:8

3. In the house of the righteous is much treasure: but in the revenues of the wicked is trouble. Proverbs 15:6

D. Is Ruled by Sin

1. His own iniquities shall take the wicked himself, and he shall be holden with the cords of his sins. Proverbs 5:22

2. The labour of the righteous tendeth to life: the fruit of the wicked to sin. Proverbs 10:16

3. The righteousness of the perfect shall direct his way: but the wicked shall fall by his own wickedness. Proverbs 11:5

E. Is Not Remembered

The memory of the just is blessed: but the name of the wicked shall rot. Proverbs 10:7

F. Is Not Worth Much

The tongue of the just is as choice silver: the heart of the wicked is little worth. Proverbs 10:20

G. Is Fearful

1. The fear of the wicked, it shall come upon him:

but the desire of the righteous shall be granted. Proverbs 10:24

2. The wicked flee when no man pursueth: but the righteous are bold as a lion. Proverbs 28:1

H. Has a Shortened Life

The fear of the LORD prolongeth days: but the years of the wicked shall be shortened. Proverbs 10:27

I. Does Not Receive His Desires

1. His own iniquities shall take the wicked himself, and he shall be holden with the cords of his sins. Proverbs 5:22

2. The LORD will not suffer the soul of the righteous to famish: but he casteth away the substance of the wicked. Proverbs 10:3

3. When a wicked man dieth, his expectation shall perish: and the hope of unjust men perisheth. Proverbs 11:7

4. The desire of the righteous is only good: but the expectation of the wicked is wrath. Proverbs 11:23

J. Receives Punishment

Though hand join in hand, the wicked shall not be unpunished: but the seed of the righteous shall be delivered. Proverbs 11:21

K. Is Repaid His Wickedness

Behold, the righteous shall be recompensed in the earth: much more the wicked and the sinner. Proverbs 11:31

L. Is Condemned of the Lord

1. A good man obtaineth favour of the LORD: but a man of wicked devices will he condemn. Proverbs 12:2

2. The righteous man wisely considereth the house of the wicked: but God overthroweth the wicked for their wickedness. Proverbs 21:12

M. Has No Stability

1. A man shall not be established by wickedness: but the root of the righteous shall not be moved. Proverbs 12:3

2. The wicked are overthrown, and are not: but the house of the righteous shall stand. Proverbs 12:7
3. Righteousness keepeth him that is upright in the way: but wickedness overthroweth the sinner. Proverbs 13:6
4. The house of the wicked shall be overthrown: but the tabernacle of the upright shall flourish. Proverbs 14:11

N. Is Trapped by What He Says

The wicked is snared by the transgression of his lips: but the just shall come out of trouble. Proverbs 12:13

O. Is Filled with Mischief

1. There shall no evil happen to the just: but the wicked shall be filled with mischief. Proverbs 12:21
2. A wicked messenger falleth into mischief: but a faithful ambassador is health. Proverbs 13:17
3. For a just man falleth seven times, and riseth up again: but the wicked shall fall into mischief. Proverbs 24:16

P. Comes to Shame

A righteous man hateth lying: but a wicked man is loathsome, and cometh to shame. Proverbs 13:5

Q. Is Unhappy

The light of the righteous rejoiceth: but the lamp of the wicked shall be put out. Proverbs 13:9

R. Lacks Food

The righteous eateth to the satisfying of his soul: but the belly of the wicked shall want. Proverbs 13:25

S. Is Hated

He that is soon angry dealeth foolishly: and a man of wicked devices is hated. Proverbs 14:17

T. Is Humbled before the Righteous

1. The evil bow before the good; and the wicked at the gates of the righteous. Proverbs 14:19
2. The wicked shall be a ransom for the righteous,

and the transgressor for the upright.
Proverbs 21:18

U. Is an Abomination to the Lord in His Way

The way of the wicked is an abomination unto the LORD: but he loveth him that followeth after righteousness. Proverbs 15:9

V. Is an Abomination to the Lord in His Sacrifices

1. The sacrifice of the wicked is an abomination to the LORD: but the prayer of the upright is his delight. Proverbs 15:8

2. The sacrifice of the wicked is abomination: how much more, when he bringeth it with a wicked mind? Proverbs 21:27

W. Is an Abomination to the Lord in His Thoughts

The thoughts of the wicked are an abomination to the LORD: but the words of the pure are pleasant words. Proverbs 15:26

X. Is Far from the Lord

The LORD is far from the wicked: but he heareth the prayer of the righteous. Proverbs 15:29

Y. Is Scattered by a Wise King

A wise king scattereth the wicked, and bringeth the wheel over them. Proverbs 20:26

IV. Warnings against the Wicked Man

A. Enter Not into the Path of the Wicked

Enter not into the path of the wicked, and go not in the way of evil men. Proverbs 4:14

B. It Is Not Good to Accept the Person of the Wicked

It is not good to accept the person of the wicked, to overthrow the righteous in judgment. Proverbs 18:5

C. Do Not Envy the Wicked

Fret not thyself because of evil men, neither be thou envious at the wicked; Proverbs 24:19

D. Never Call a Wicked Man Righteous

He that saith unto the wicked, Thou art righteous; him shall the people curse, nations shall abhor him: Proverbs 24:24

Chapter 11

THE JUST MAN

Proverbs 24:16
For a just man falleth seven
times, and riseth up again: but
the wicked shall fall into mischief.

In contrast to the Wicked Man is the Just Man. Many of the characteristics of the Just Man are similar to those of the Righteous Man. His most outstanding attribute is that he is fair and treats all equally. A Just Man has the ability to make proper decisions. He would act in an equitable manner in the position of a judge and honest in the duties of a police officer. Anyone in authority needs to posses the characteristics of the Just Man. A Just Man will be impartial in his judgments and will not hesitate to pronounce a verdict against sin. The Just Man may have to make a decision concerning someone he loves, but he will not let a relationship keep him from doing what is right.

Though the Just Man is a very blessed man, there is a price to pay. Evil doers often dislike those who are just. However, the eternal reward will far exceed the earthly discomfort.

The Just Man

Dictionary "JUST": Righteous, religious; influenced by a regard to the laws of God; or living in exact conformity to the divine will.

Hebrew "JUST": To be right; lawful (6663); righteous; one with equity(6662); uprightness.

I.   Actions of the Just Man
A.   Learns What He Is Taught

Cornelius
Acts 10:22-48

> Give instruction to a wise man, and he will be yet wiser: teach a just man, and he will increase in learning. Proverbs 9:9

B.   Walks in His Integrity

Joseph
Matthew 1:19

> The just man walketh in his integrity: his children are blessed after him. Proverbs 20:7
> Dictionary "INTEGRITY": completeness, innocence, uprightness.

C.   Is Glad to Pronounce a Verdict to Provide Justice

Samuel
I Samuel 15:3, 32, 33

> It is joy to the just to do judgment: but destruction shall be to the workers of iniquity.
> Proverbs 21:15

II. Characteristics of the Just Man
A. Has Speech Worth Hearing

Solomon
I Kings 3:16-28;
I Kings 10:1-7

1. The tongue of the just is as choice silver: the heart of the wicked is little worth. Proverbs 10:20
2. The mouth of the just bringeth forth wisdom: but the froward tongue shall be cut out. Proverbs 10:31

B. Rises Up Again When He Falls

Job
Job 23:10-17

For a just man falleth seven times, and riseth up again: but the wicked shall fall into mischief. Proverbs 24:16

C. Is Not Friends with an Unjust Man
(his best friend is not an ungodly man)

Moses
Numbers 16:1-15

An unjust man is an abomination to the just: and he that is upright in the way is abomination to the wicked. Proverbs 29:27

III. Rewards of the Just Man
A. His Children Are Blessed (happy)
The just man walketh in his integrity: his children are blessed after him. Proverbs 20:7
B. His Home Is Blessed (prosperous)
The curse of the LORD is in the house of the wicked: but he blesseth the habitation of the just. Proverbs 3:33

C. **He Himself Is Blessed** (prosperous)

Blessings are upon the head of the just: but violence covereth the mouth of the wicked. Proverbs 10:6

D. **The Memory of Him is Blessed**
(Benediction; prosperity)

The memory of the just is blessed: but the name of the wicked shall rot. Proverbs 10:7

E. **He is Kept from Trouble**

1. An hypocrite with his mouth destroyeth his neighbour: but through knowledge shall the just be delivered. Proverbs 11:9

2. The wicked is snared by the transgression of his lips: but the just shall come out of trouble. Proverbs 12:13

3. There shall no evil happen to the just: but the wicked shall be filled with mischief. Proverbs 12:21

F. **He Receives the Sinner's Wealth**

A good man leaveth an inheritance to his children's children: and the wealth of the sinner is laid up for the just. Proverbs 13:22

G. **His Enemies Are an Abomination to God**

He that justifieth the wicked, and he that condemneth the just, even they both are abomination to the LORD. Proverbs 17:15

Dictionary "CONDEMN": to be (cause, do, or declare) wrong

Chapter 12

THE RIGHTEOUS MAN

Proverbs 28:12
When righteous men do rejoice, there
is great glory: but when the wicked
rise, a man is hidden.

The Righteous Man is the opposite of the Wicked Man. The Righteous Man is not only saved, but is also obedient to God's commands. Because of his willingness to live his life in accordance to the Bible, he receives all the blessings that are promised as a result of it. Consequently, he is happy and prosperous. The Righteous Man grows in grace daily.

The Righteous Man

Dictionary "RIGHTEOUS": Just; according to the divine law. Denotes one who is holy in heart, and observant of the divine commands in practice.

Hebrew "RIGHTEOUS": To be right, just, lawful (6662).

I. Actions of the Righteous Man
A. Has Good Desires

Paul
Romans 10:1

> The desire of the righteous is only good: but the expectation of the wicked is wrath.
> Proverbs 11:23

B. Has Right Thoughts

Joseph
Genesis 50:15-21

> The thoughts of the righteous are right: but the counsels of the wicked are deceit.
> Proverbs 12:5

C. Regards the Life of Animals

David
I Samuel 17:34-36

> A righteous man regardeth the life of his beast: but the tender mercies of the wicked are cruel.
> Proverbs 12:10

86

D. Speaks the Truth

Micaiah
I Kings 22:13-28

> He that speaketh truth sheweth forth righteousness: but a false witness deceit. Proverbs 12:17

E. Hates Lying

Jeremiah
Jeremiah 28:15-17

> A righteous man hateth lying: but a wicked man is loathsome, and cometh to shame. Proverbs 13:5

F. Fears God

Abraham
Genesis 22:12

> He that walketh in his uprightness feareth the LORD: but he that is perverse in his ways despiseth him. Proverbs 14:2

G. Studies to Be Able to Answer

Shadrach, Meshach,
& Abednego
Daniel 3:16

> The heart of the righteous studieth to answer: but the mouth of the wicked poureth out evil things. Proverbs 15:28

H. Departs from Evil

Job
Job 1:8; 2:3

The highway of the upright is to depart from evil: he that keepeth his way preserveth his soul. Proverbs 16:17

I. Is Pure

Joseph
Matthew 1:19

The way of man is froward and strange: but as for the pure, his work is right. Proverbs 21:8

J. Considers the House of the Wicked

Solomon
I Kings 2:36-46

The righteous man wisely considereth the house of the wicked: but God overthroweth the wicked for their wickedness. Proverbs 21:12

K. Is a Giver

Barnabas
Acts 4:36, 37

He coveteth greedily all the day long: but the righteous giveth and spareth not. Proverbs 21:26

L. Sings and Rejoices

Asaph
Psalm 81:1-4

In the transgression of an evil man there is a snare: but the righteous doth sing and rejoice. Proverbs 29:6

M. Considers the Poor

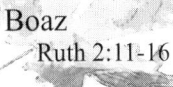

Boaz
Ruth 2:11-16

The righteous considereth the cause of the poor: but the wicked regardeth not to know it. Proverbs 29:7

II. Rewards of the Righteous Man
A. Is Shielded by God
He layeth up sound wisdom for the righteous: he is a buckler to them that walk uprightly. Proverbs 2:7

B. Has Satisfaction from God
1. The LORD will not suffer the soul of the righteous to famish: but he casteth away the substance of the wicked. Proverbs 10:3
2. The righteous eateth to the satisfying of his soul: but the belly of the wicked shall want. Proverbs 13:25

C. Has Confidence
1. He that walketh uprightly walketh surely: but he that perverteth his ways shall be known. Proverbs 10:9
2. The name of the LORD is a strong tower: the righteous runneth into it, and is safe. Proverbs 18:10

D. Has Desires Granted
The fear of the wicked, it shall come upon him: but the desire of the righteous shall be granted. Proverbs 10:24

E. Has a Strong Foundation
1. As the whirlwind passeth, so is the wicked no more: but the righteous is an everlasting

foundation. Proverbs 10:25

2. The righteous shall never be removed: but the wicked shall not inhabit the earth. Proverbs 10:30

3. A man shall not be established by wickedness: but the root of the righteous shall not be moved. Proverbs 12:3

4. The wicked are overthrown, and are not: but the house of the righteous shall stand. Proverbs 12:7

5. The wicked desireth the net of evil men: but the root of the righteous yieldeth fruit. Proverbs 12:12

F. Receives Gladness

1. The hope of the righteous shall be gladness: but the expectation of the wicked shall perish. Proverbs 10:28

2. The light of the righteous rejoiceth: but the lamp of the wicked shall be put out. Proverbs 13:9

G. Has Direction

1. The integrity of the upright shall guide them: but the perverseness of transgressors shall destroy them. Proverbs 11:3

2. The righteousness of the perfect shall direct his way: but the wicked shall fall by his own wickedness. Proverbs 11:5

3. A man's heart deviseth his way: but the LORD directeth his steps. Proverbs 16:9

4. A wicked man hardeneth his face: but as for the upright, he directeth his way. Proverbs 21:29

H. Is Delivered out of Trouble

1. The righteous is delivered out of trouble, and the wicked cometh in his stead. Proverbs 11:8

2. The wicked shall be a ransom for the righteous, and the transgressor for the upright. Proverbs 21:18

I. Has a Sure Reward

The wicked worketh a deceitful work: but to him that soweth righteousness shall be a sure reward. Proverbs 11:18

J. Delights God

1. They that are of a froward heart are abomination to the LORD: but such as are upright in their way are his delight. Proverbs 11:20

2. Yea, my reins shall rejoice, when thy lips speak right things. Proverbs 23:16

K. Is Repayed

1. Behold, the righteous shall be recompensed in the earth: much more the wicked and the sinner. Proverbs 11:31

2. Evil pursueth sinners: but to the righteous good shall be repayed. Proverbs 13:21

L. Is Favoured

1. The righteous is more excellent than his neighbour: but the way of the wicked seduceth them. Proverbs 12:26

2. Fools make a mock at sin: but among the righteous there is favour. Proverbs 14:9

3. When righteous men do rejoice, there is great glory: but when the wicked rise, a man is hidden. Proverbs 28:12

M. Has Riches

In the house of the righteous is much treasure: but in the revenues of the wicked is trouble. Proverbs 15:6

N. Is Loved by God

The way of the wicked is an abomination unto the LORD: but he loveth him that followeth after righteousness. Proverbs 15:9

O. Has Understanding

Folly is joy to him that is destitute of wisdom: but a man of understanding walketh uprightly. Proverbs 15:21

P. Has Answered Prayer

1. The sacrifice of the wicked is an abomination to the LORD: but the prayer of the upright is his delight. Proverbs 15:8

2. The LORD is far from the wicked: but he heareth the prayer of the righteous. Proverbs 15:29

Q. Is Loved by Authority

Righteous lips are the delight of kings; and they love him that speaketh right. Proverbs 16:13

R. Finds Life, Righteousness, and Honour

He that followeth after righteousness and mercy findeth life, righteousness, and honour. Proverbs 21:21

S. Pleases His Father

The father of the righteous shall greatly rejoice: and he that begetteth a wise child shall have joy of him. Proverbs 23:24

T. Is Bold

The wicked flee when no man pursueth: but the righteous are bold as a lion. Proverbs 28:1

U. Has Good Things

Whoso causeth the righteous to go astray in an evil way, he shall fall himself into his own pit: but the upright shall have good things in possession. Proverbs 28:10

V. Is Alert to Sin

When the wicked are multiplied, transgression increaseth: but the righteous shall see their fall. Proverbs 29:16

Chapter 13

THE YOUNG MAN

Proverbs 1:4
To give subtilty to the simple,
to the young man knowledge
and discretion.

The Young Man, who is the opposite of the Old Man, is simply a person in the early part of his life.

In the Bible, people are not classified as old because they have reached a certain age. When God spoke to the Israelites through Moses, He spoke of the children as those under twenty. When the Children of Israel wandered in the wilderness for forty years, the ones who were allowed to enter the Promised Land were those who were nineteen and younger, or the "... little ones ... " Numbers 14:29-33.

The main characteristic that should be remembered in connection with the Young Man is that he is without understanding. The influences to which he is subject will invariably be what establishes his ideals and opinions. The book of Proverbs was particularly written to the young man. Proverbs 1:4 says, "To give subtilty to the simple, to the young man knowledge and discretion."

The Young Man

Dictionary "YOUNG": Not having been long born; being in the first part of life; not old; ignorant; having little experience.

Hebrew "YOUNG": A boy (5288); a youth (970).

Characteristics of the Young Man
A.   The Young Man Needs Knowledge and Discretion

Josiah
II Kings 22:1-20

> To give subtilty to the simple, to the young man knowledge and discretion. Proverbs 1:4

B.   The Young Man Is without Understanding

Rich Young Ruler
Matthew 19:16-22

> And beheld among the simple ones, I discerned among the youths, a young man void of understanding, Proverbs 7:7

C.   The Glory of a Young Man Is His Strength

David
I Samuel 16:12-18

> The glory of young men is their strength: and the beauty of old men is the gray head.
> Proverbs 20:29

Chapter 14

THE OLD MAN

Proverbs 20:29
The glory of young men is their
strength: and the beauty of
old men is the gray head.

Opposite the Young Man is the Old Man. The Old Man is often expected to have wisdom to match his years. This, however, is not always the case. "The hoary head is a crown of glory, if it be found in the way of righteousness." Proverbs 16:31. The condition in this verse explains why many older people are not wise.

The Old Man may have lived a righteous or a wicked life. Whichever life he has chosen, he will always reap what he sows.

The Old Man

Dictionary "OLD": Advanced far in years or life.

Hebrew "OLD": to be old, aged man (2204).

I. Characteristics of the Old Man
A. The Gray Head is a Beauty to Old Men

David
Psalm 71:17-18

The glory of young men is their strength: and the beauty of old men is the gray head.
Proverbs 20:29

B. An Old Man Will Not Depart from Right, If He Is Trained as a Child

Samuel
I Samuel 12:1-4

Train up a child in the way he should go: and when he is old, he will not depart from it.
Proverbs 22:6

II. Warning Concerning the Old Man
Disrespect Should Not Be Shown to Old Men

Hearken unto thy father that begat thee, and despise not thy mother when she is old.
Proverbs 23:22
Dictionary "DESPISE": disrespect, shamed.

III. Reward for the Old Man
Grandchildren Are a Crown to Old Men

Children's children are the crown of old men; and the glory of children are their fathers.
Proverbs 17:6

Chapter 15

THE EVIL MAN

Proverbs 17:11
An evil man seeketh only rebellion:
therefore a cruel messenger shall be
sent against him.

The Evil Man is the opposite of the Good Man. The Evil Man is saved, but would probably not be recognized as such because of his backslidden condition. His characteristics are similar to those of the Wicked Man. Although he will go to Heaven, he will act like a heathen on this earth. Proverbs 2:13 describes Evil Men as those "Who leave the paths of uprightness..." In order to leave something, a person must have been there at one time. The verse goes on to say, ". . . to walk in the ways of darkness;" This shows the Evil Man walking and living as the unsaved man (Wicked Man). How many times do soul winners meet people who claim to be saved though their lives belie their words? They are either baby Christians who never grew up in the Lord, or seasoned Christians who have turned away from the Lord.

Just as God gave a warning concerning the Wicked Man, he has also issued a warning concerning the Evil Man. Many Christian parents inadvertently allow their children to associate with backslidden Christians. The parents might make the excuse that at least the companions of their children are saved. If the truth were known; however, the saved, but backslidden, evil crowd may cause more damage than the unsaved, wicked crowd.

The Evil Man

Dictionary "EVIL": Any deviation of a moral agent from the rules of conduct prescribed to him by God or by legitimate human authority.

Hebrew "EVIL": Bad or evil, wretchedness, wrong (7451).

I.   Actions of the Evil Man
A.   Speaks Frowardly

Shimei
II Samuel 16:5-8

> To deliver thee from the way of the evil man, from the man that speaketh froward things; Proverbs 2:12

B.   Leaves the Paths of Uprightness

Demas
II Timothy 4:10

> Who leave the paths of uprightness, to walk in the ways of darkness; Proverbs 2:13

C.   Rejoices to Do Evil

Judah & Israel
Jeremiah 11:14-17

> Who rejoice to do evil, and delight in the frowardness of the wicked; Proverbs 2:14

D.   Delights in the Frowardness of the Wicked

Lot
Genesis 13:10-13;
19:1

Who rejoice to do evil, and delight in the frowardness of the wicked; Proverbs 2:14

E. Seeks Rebellion

Saul
I Samuel 15:22-23

An evil man seeketh only rebellion: therefore a cruel messenger shall be sent against him. Proverbs 17:11

II. Characteristics of the Evil Man
A. Has Crooked and Froward Ways

Manasseh
II Kings 21:1-9

Whose ways are crooked, and they froward in their paths: Proverbs 2:15

B. Does Not See His Wrong

Samson
Judges 16:4-20

Evil men understand not judgment: but they that seek the LORD understand all things.
Proverbs 28:5

III. Consequences of the Evil Man
A. Dies
As righteousness tendeth to life: so he that pursueth evil pursueth it to his own death. Proverbs 11:19
B. Bows (humbled) before the Good
The evil bow before the good; and the wicked at the gates of the righteous. Proverbs 14:19

C. Has No Reward

> Fret not thyself because of evil men, neither be thou envious at the wicked; For there shall be no reward to the evil man; the candle of the wicked shall be put out. Proverbs 24:19-20

D. Is Trapped

> In the transgression of an evil man there is a snare: but the righteous doth sing and rejoice. Proverbs 29:6

IV. Warnings Against the Evil Man

A. Do Not be With Him

1. Turn not to the right hand nor to the left: remove thy foot from evil. Proverbs 4:27
2. Be not thou envious against evil men, neither desire to be with them. Proverbs 24:1

B. Do Not be Envious of Him

> Be not thou envious against evil men, neither desire to be with them. Proverbs 24:1

C. Do Not Anger Yourself Because of Him

> Fret not thyself because of evil men, neither be thou envious at the wicked; Proverbs 24:19

Chapter 16

THE GOOD MAN

Proverbs 12:2
A good man obtaineth favour of
the LORD: but a man of wicked
devices will he condemn.

The Good Man is the opposite of the Evil Man, not only in action, but also in attitude. The Good Man will make an attempt to help others and to guide his actions with the golden rule "do unto others as you would have them do unto you," or "love thy neighbor as thyself."

The most prevalent action of the Good Man is his constant effort to improve. He never becomes complacent with his progress. He realizes that there is something to be learned from everyone, and he is willing to learn it.

In contrast to the Evil Man, the Good Man is very well liked. Naturally, people prefer the company of the Good Man to that of the Evil Man. Because of his good characteristics, people do not hesitate to do things for him. They are confident that he is deserving and that he would not hesitate to do the same for others.

The Good Man

Dictionary "GOOD": Having moral qualities best adapted to its design and use, or the qualities which God's law requires.

Hebrew "GOOD": Good, pleasant, glad (2896).

I. Actions of the Good Man
A. Leaves an Inheritance to His Grandchildren

Job
Job 42:13-17

A good man leaveth an inheritance to his children's children: and the wealth of the sinner is laid up for the just. Proverbs 13:22

B. Is Always Trying to Improve

Paul
Philippians 3:12-14

The backslider in heart shall be filled with his own ways: and a good man shall be satisfied from himself. Proverbs 14:14

C. Handles a Matter Wisely

David
I Samuel 18:5, 14-15

He that handleth a matter wisely shall find good: and whoso trusteth in the LORD, happy is he. Proverbs 16:20

D. Keeps Understanding

Ezra
Ezra 7:10

He that getteth wisdom loveth his own soul: he that keepeth understanding shall find good. Proverbs 19:8

II. Characteristics of the Good Man
A. Does Not Have a Froward Heart

John the Baptist
Luke 3:2-8

He that hath a froward heart findeth no good: and he that hath a perverse tongue falleth into mischief. Proverbs 17:20

B. Does Not Show Partiality

Jesus
Mark 12:14

1. These things also belong to the wise. It is not good to have respect of persons in judgment. Proverbs 24:23
2. To have respect of persons is not good: for for a piece of bread that man will transgress. Proverbs 28:21

III. Rewards of the Good Man
A. Receives Favour from Others
He that diligently seeketh good procureth favour: but he that seeketh mischief, it shall come unto him. Proverbs 11:27
B. Has Favour with the Lord
A good man obtaineth favour of the LORD: but a man of wicked devices will he condemn. Proverbs 12:2
C. Humbles the Evil
The evil bow before the good; and the wicked at the gates of the righteous. Proverbs 14:19

D.   Receives Mercy and Truth

> Do they not err that devise evil? but mercy and truth shall be to them that devise good.
> Proverbs 14:22

Chapter 17

THE ANGRY MAN

Proverbs 22:24
Make no friendship with an angry
man; and with a furious man thou
shalt not go:

Since the Angry Man is the opposite of the Discreet Man, he uses no discretion in his actions.

The Angry Man has no control over his temper. Although there is a time to be angry, the Angry Man does not know when that time is. As opposed to the righteous indignation of the Discreet Man, the Angry Man displays a lack of self-control. An Angry Man will react to a situation rather than acting upon it. The Angry Man's actions may have a domino effect. For instance; dad yells at mom, mom spanks the kids, the kids kick the dog, and the dog bites the cat.

A Discreet Man will not allow the attitude of one person to change his actions. The Angry Man needs to ask God daily for patience.

The Angry Man

Dictionary "ANGRY": A violent passion of the mind excited by a real or supposed injury; usually accompanied with the propensity to take vengeance, or to obtain satisfaction from the offending party.

Hebrew "ANGRY": To breathe hard, be enraged (599); to foam at the mouth, abhor (2194).

I. Actions of the Angry Man
A. Deals Foolishly

Asa
II Chronicles 16:7-10

1. A fool's wrath is presently known: but a prudent man covereth shame. Proverbs 12:16
2. He that is soon angry dealeth foolishly: and a man of wicked devices is hated. Proverbs 14:17
3. He that is slow to wrath is of great understanding: but he that is hasty of spirit exalteth folly. Proverbs 14:29
4. A stone is heavy, and the sand weighty; but a fool's wrath is heavier than them both. Proverbs 27:3

B. Causes Others to Be Angry

Saul
I Samuel 20:30-34

1. The north wind driveth away rain: so doth an angry countenance a backbiting tongue. Proverbs 25:23
2. An angry man stirreth up strife, and a furious man aboundeth in transgression. Proverbs 29:22

II. Characteristics of the Angry Man
A. Is Scornful

Cain
Genesis 4:4-10

1. Proud and haughty scorner is his name, who dealeth in proud wrath. Proverbs 21:24
2. Scornful men bring a city into a snare: but wise men turn away wrath. Proverbs 29:8

B. Abounds in Sin

Uzziah
II Chronicles 26:16-21

1. A man of great wrath shall suffer punishment: for if thou deliver him, yet thou must do it again. Proverbs 19:19
2. An angry man stirreth up strife, and a furious man aboundeth in transgression. Proverbs 29:22

C. Lacks Understanding

Nebuchadnezzar
Daniel 3:13-30

He that is slow to wrath is of great understanding: but he that is hasty of spirit exalteth folly. Proverbs 14:29

III. Warnings Against the Angry Man
A. Do Not Make Friends with Him

Make no friendship with an angry man; and with a furious man thou shalt not go: Lest thou learn his ways, and get a snare to thy soul. Proverbs 22:24, 25

B. Avoid Him
> Make no friendship with an angry man; and with a furious man thou shalt not go: Proverbs 22:24

Chapter 18

THE DISCREET MAN

Proverbs 19:11
The discretion of a man deferreth his anger; and it is his glory to pass over a transgression.

As opposed to the Angry Man, the Discreet Man is not at the mercy of his surroundings to determine whether or not he will become angry. People and circumstances are not deciding factors for the Discreet Man.

God said in Ephesians 4:26, "Be ye angry, and sin not . . . " The Discreet Man realizes that there is a time and a place for anger. Jesus demonstrated this principle when He became angry with the money changers in the temple.

The word "discreet" in Hebrew means "a plan of thought." The Discreet Man has already planned what things should make him angry before he becomes angry. He handles each situation with discretion.

The Discreet Man

Dictionary "DISCREET": To separate; to see or understand the difference.

Hebrew "DISCREET":   A plan, thought (4209); perception, intelligence, reason (2940).

I.   Characteristics of the Discreet Man
A.   Discretion is Needed by the Young Man

Joseph
   Genesis 41:33, 39

> To give subtilty to the simple, to the young man knowledge and discretion. Proverbs 1:4

B.   Discretion May be Lost; It Must be Maintained

Daniel
   Daniel 6:2-10

> 1.   My son, let not them depart from thine eyes: keep sound wisdom and discretion: Proverbs 3:21
> 2.   That thou mayest regard discretion, and that thy lips may keep knowledge. Proverbs 5:2

C.   Discretion Surpasses Outward Beauty

Job
   Job 30:30-31:7

> As a jewel of gold in a swine's snout, so is a fair woman which is without discretion.
> Proverbs 11:22

II. Rewards of the Discreet Man

A. He Will Be Preserved

Discretion shall preserve thee, understanding shall keep thee: Proverbs 2:11

Dictionary "PRESERVE": to hedge about, guard, or protect

B. He Will Have His Anger Deferred

The discretion of a man deferreth his anger; and it is his glory to pass over a transgression. Proverbs 19:11

Dictionary "DEFERRETH": to be long; to draw out or lengthen.

Chapter 19

THE FROWARD MAN

Proverbs 16:28
A froward man soweth strife: and a
whisperer separateth chief friends.

The Froward Man is not only the opposite of the Upright Man, but he is also the same as the Perverse Man. A Froward Man can be pictured as one who travels a crooked path instead of a straight one. He is perverse and disobedient.

He is characterized by froward talk, a froward walk, froward thoughts, and a froward heart. A man does not become froward overnight. The frowardness begins in his heart and eventually filters into his thoughts, his conversations, and then his actions.

A person can be saved or lost and still be froward. If a man is saved and is froward, he is most definitely in a backslidden condition. The backslidden Christian will become even more froward due to his coldness to Christ.

The Froward (Perverse) Man

Dictionary "FROWARD": Turned or looking from, not willing to yield or comply with what is required.

Hebrew "FROWARD": A perversity or fraud (8419), distorted, hence false, crooked (6141).

Dictionary "PERVERSE": 1. Turned aside, distorted from the right (saved). 2. Obstinate in the wrong, stubborn (unsaved).

I. Actions of the Froward Man
A. Despises the Lord

Belshazzar
  Daniel 5:17-31

> 1. He that walketh in his uprightness feareth the LORD: but he that is perverse in his ways despiseth him. Proverbs 14:2
> 2. The foolishness of man perverteth his way: and his heart fretteth against the LORD. Proverbs 19:3

B. Sows Strife

Doeg
  I Samuel 22:9-18

> A froward man soweth strife: and a whisperer separateth chief friends. Proverbs 16:28

C. Is Foolish

Saul
  I Samuel 13:11-14

> The foolishness of man perverteth his way: and

his heart fretteth against the LORD.
Proverbs 19:3

II. Characteristics of the Froward Man
A. Froward Talk

Shimei
II Samuel 16:5-9

1.   To deliver thee from the way of the evil man, from the man that speaketh froward things;
Proverbs 2:12
2.   Put away from thee a froward mouth, and perverse lips put far from thee.
Proverbs 4:24
3.   A naughty person, a wicked man, walketh with a froward mouth. Proverbs 6:12
4.   All the words of my mouth are in righteousness; there is nothing froward or perverse in them.
Proverbs 8:8
5.   The fear of the LORD is to hate evil: pride, and arrogancy, and the evil way, and the froward mouth, do I hate. Proverbs 8:13
6.   The mouth of the just bringeth forth wisdom: but the froward tongue shall be cut out.
Proverbs 10:31
7.   The lips of the righteous know what is acceptable: but the mouth of the wicked speaketh frowardness. Proverbs 10:32
8.   A wholesome tongue is a tree of life: but perverseness therein is a breach in the spirit.
Proverbs 15:4
9.   He that hath a froward heart findeth no good: and he that hath a perverse tongue falleth into mischief. Proverbs 17:20
10. Better is the poor that walketh in his integrity, than he that is perverse in his lips, and is a fool.
Proverbs 19:1

B. Froward Walk

Samson
Judges 16

1. Who rejoice to do evil, and delight in the frowardness of the wicked; Whose ways are crooked, and they froward in their paths: Proverbs 2:14-15
2. He that walketh in his uprightness feareth the LORD: but he that is perverse in his ways despiseth him. Proverbs 14:2
3. The way of man is froward and strange: but as for the pure, his work is right. Proverbs 21:8
4. Thorns and snares are in the way of the froward: he that doth keep his soul shall be far from them. Proverbs 22:5
5. Better is the poor that walketh in his uprightness, than he that is perverse in his ways, though he be rich. Proverbs 28:6

C. Froward Thoughts

Amnon
II Samuel 13:1-15

He shutteth his eyes to devise froward things: moving his lips he bringeth evil to pass. Proverbs 16:30

D. Froward Heart

Wicked
(Lost People)
Isaiah 57:17-21

1. Frowardness is in his heart, he deviseth mischief continually; he soweth discord. Proverbs 6:14

2. They that are of a froward heart are abomination to the LORD: but such as are upright in their way are his delight. Proverbs 11:20
3. A man shall be commended according to his wisdom: but he that is of a perverse heart shall be despised. Proverbs 12:8
4. He that hath a froward heart findeth no good: and he that hath a perverse tongue falleth into mischief. Proverbs 17:20
5. Thine eyes shall behold strange women, and thine heart shall utter perverse things. Proverbs 23:33

III. The Consequences of a Froward Man
A. Is Despised
A man shall be commended according to his wisdom: but he that is of a perverse heart shall be despised. Proverbs 12:8
B. Finds No Good
He that hath a froward heart findeth no good: and he that hath a perverse tongue falleth into mischief. Proverbs 17:20
C. Falls into Mischief
He that hath a froward heart findeth no good: and he that hath a perverse tongue falleth into mischief. Proverbs 17:20
D. Is an Abomination to the Lord
1. For the froward is abomination to the LORD: but his secret is with the righteous. Proverbs 3:32
2. They that are of a froward heart are abomination to the LORD: but such as are upright in their way are his delight. Proverbs 11:20
E. Falls at Once
Whoso walketh uprightly shall be saved: but he that is perverse in his ways shall fall at once. Proverbs 28:18
F. Is Destroyed
The integrity of the upright shall guide them: but the perverseness of transgressors shall destroy them. Proverbs 11:3

G. Has a Broken Spirit

A wholesome tongue is a tree of life: but perverseness therein is a breach in the spirit. Proverbs 15:4

H. Is a Public Disgrace

He that walketh uprightly walketh surely: but he that perverteth his ways shall be known. Proverbs 10:9

Chapter 20

THE UPRIGHT MAN

Proverbs 29:27
An unjust man is an abomination to
the just: and he that is upright in the
way is abomination to the wicked.

The Upright Man is a combination of the Righteous Man and the Just Man. He is the extreme opposite of the Froward Man. The Upright Man is honest and straightforward. He treats all equally and is fair in his judgments. He has a personal relationship with the Lord and is concerned with pleasing Him.

The Upright Man is pleasant to be around. The Upright Man is often the cause of God's blessings on those around him. God blessed Potiphar's house for Joseph's sake (Gen. 39:5). Potiphar was not upright but Joseph was, yet both of them were blessed.

Wise is the employer who employs upright Christians. The Upright Man lives a consistent, Christ-honoring life.

The Upright Man

Dictionary "UPRIGHT":   Honest; just; not deviating from correct moral principles.

Hebrew "UPRIGHT":   Straight; equity; just, right (3477).

I.   Actions of the Upright Man
A.   Goes the Way of the Lord

Samuel
  I Samuel 2:18-26;
  3:10-19

> The way of the LORD is strength to the upright: but destruction shall be to the workers of iniquity. Proverbs 10:29

B.   Departs from Evil

David
  II Samuel 22:24

> The highway of the upright is to depart from evil: he that keepeth his way preserveth his soul. Proverbs 16:17

C.   Directs His Way (to set up; plan)

Nehemiah
  Nehemiah 2:11-18

> A wicked man hardeneth his face: but as for the upright, he directeth his way.   Proverbs 21:29

II.   Characteristics of the Upright Man
A.   Is Guided by His Integrity

Job
  Job 2:3

The integrity of the upright shall guide them: but the perverseness of transgressors shall destroy them. Proverbs 11:3

B. Is Delivered by His Righteousness

Shadrach, Meshach,
and Abednego
Daniel 3:16-28

1. The righteousness of the upright shall deliver them: but transgressors shall be taken in their own naughtiness. Proverbs 11:6
2. Righteousness keepeth him that is upright in the way: but wickedness overthroweth the sinner. Proverbs 13:6

C. Exalts the City Because He Is Blessed

Joseph
Genesis 39:5, 23;
41:33-44

By the blessing of the upright the city is exalted: but it is overthrown by the mouth of the wicked. Proverbs 11:11

III. Rewards of the Upright Man

A. Dwells in the Land

For the upright shall dwell in the land, and the perfect shall remain in it. Proverbs 2:21

B. Is Strengthened

The way of the LORD is strength to the upright: but destruction shall be to the workers of iniquity. Proverbs 10:29

C. Is Guided

The integrity of the upright shall guide them: but the perverseness of transgressors shall destroy them. Proverbs 11:3

D. Is Delivered

1. The righteousness of the upright shall deliver

them: but transgressors shall be taken in their own naughtiness. Proverbs 11:6

2. The words of the wicked are to lie in wait for blood: but the mouth of the upright shall deliver them. Proverbs 12:6

E. Is Blessed

By the blessing of the upright the city is exalted: but it is overthrown by the mouth of the wicked. Proverbs 11:11

F. Delights the Lord

1. They that are of a froward heart are abomination to the LORD: but such as are upright in their way are his delight. Proverbs 11:20

2. The sacrifice of the wicked is an abomination to the LORD: but the prayer of the upright is his delight. Proverbs 15:8

G. Is Guarded or Protected

Righteousness keepeth him that is upright in the way: but wickedness overthroweth the sinner. Proverbs 13:6

H. Flourishes

The house of the wicked shall be overthrown: but the tabernacle of the upright shall flourish. Proverbs 14:11

I. Possesses Good Things

Whoso causeth the righteous to go astray in an evil way, he shall fall himself into his own pit: but the upright shall have good things in possession. Proverbs 28:10

Chapter 21

THE CONTENTIOUS MAN

Proverbs 26:21
As coals are to burning coals, and
wood to fire; so is a contentious man
to kindle strife.

The Contentious Man can be described as one who causes strife. The book of Proverbs has a formula for the cause of strife; pride (13:10) + contention (17:14) = strife. The two addends together cause strife. If only one element is present, then strife will not be present. To have strife there must be both pride and contention. Contention is the hateful feeling that causes a quarrel when displayed.

The Contentious Man has only one action, he kindles strife. Although a variety of people can cause contention, the results are the same.

The Contentious Man

Dictionary "CONTENTIOUS": Given to angry debate; quarrelsome.

Hebrew "CONTENTIOUS": Brawling; a contest or quarrel; discord; strife.

I. Action of a Contentious Man
Kindles Strife

Sanballat
Nehemiah 4:1-3

1. The beginning of strife is as when one letteth out water: therefore leave off contention, before it be meddled with. Proverbs 17:14
2. As coals are to burning coals, and wood to fire; so is a contentious man to kindle strife. Proverbs 26:21

II. People Who Are Contentious
A. The Proud

Haman
Esther 3:5, 6

Only by pride cometh contention: but with the well advised is wisdom. Proverbs 13:10

B. The Fool

Nabal
I Samuel 25:3, 9-11, 25

A fool's lips enter into contention, and his mouth calleth for strokes. Proverbs 18:6

C. The Scorner

Ishmael
Genesis 21:9-14

> Cast out the scorner, and contention shall go out;
> yea, strife and reproach shall cease.
> Proverbs 22:10

D. The Brother Offended

Joab
(Killing Abner)
II Samuel 3:23-38

> A brother offended is harder to be won than a
> strong city: and their contentions are like the bars
> of a castle. Proverbs 18:19

E. The Drunkard

Ahasuerus
Esther 1:10-12

> Who hath woe? who hath sorrow? who hath
> contentions? who hath babbling? who hath
> wounds without cause? who hath redness of
> eyes? They that tarry long at the wine; they that go
> to seek mixed wine. Proverbs 23:29-30

F. Some Women

Jezebel
I Kings 19:1-2

> 1. It is better to dwell in the wilderness, than with a
>   contentious and an angry woman.
>   Proverbs 21:19
> 2. A continual dropping in a very rainy day and a
>   contentious woman are alike. Proverbs 27:15

G. Some Wives

Michal
II Samuel 6:16,
20-23

A foolish son is the calamity of his father: and the contentions of a wife are a continual dropping. Proverbs 19:13

Chapter 22

THE DECEITFUL MAN

Proverbs 29:13
The poor and the deceitful man meet
together: the LORD lighteneth both
their eyes.

The Deceitful Man purposely misleads people concerning his intentions. He causes those around him to trust him and to believe that his desires are wholesome and right, while his motives are far from pure. He puts on a façade of being a knight in shining armour when in reality, he is a black knight.

His front is often extremely convincing and fools even the best of men. Although the Deceitful Man is confident in the success of his act, his reckoning day is sure to come.

The Deceitful Man

Dictionary "DECEITFUL": Tending to mislead, deceive or ensnare, trickish.

Hebrew "DECEITFUL": The sense of deceiving fraud; feigned (4820); an untruth, a sham, false, liar (8267).

I.   Actions of the Deceitful Man
A.   Imagines Evil

Herod
Matthew 2:7-16

Deceit is in the heart of them that imagine evil: but to the counsellors of peace is joy.
Proverbs 12:20

B.   Is Foolish

Shemaiah
Jeremiah 29:8, 24-32

The wisdom of the prudent is to understand his way: but the folly of fools is deceit.
Proverbs 14:8
Hebrew "Folly": silliness, foolishly (200).

C.   Hates

Joseph's Brothers
Genesis 37:18-32

1.   He that hateth dissembleth with his lips, and layeth up deceit within him; Proverbs 26:24
2.   Whose hatred is covered by deceit, his wickedness shall be shewed before the whole congregation. Proverbs 26:26

D. Tears Down Others with His Lips

Satan
Genesis 3:1-5

> He that hateth dissembleth with his lips, and layeth up deceit within him; Proverbs 26:24 Dictionary "DISSEMBLETH": scrutinize, disregard, ignore.

E. Speaks Lies

Jacob
Genesis 27:1-36

1. A true witness delivereth souls: but a deceitful witness speaketh lies. Proverbs 14:25
2. Be not a witness against thy neighbour without cause; and deceive not with thy lips. Proverbs 24:28

F. Seeks Favour, Usually through Flattery

Pharisees
Matthew 22:15-22

1. Faithful are the wounds of a friend; but the kisses of an enemy are deceitful. Proverbs 27:6
2. Favour is deceitful, and beauty is vain: but a woman that feareth the LORD, she shall be praised. Proverbs 31:30

II. People Who Are Deceitful
   A. The Wicked (unsaved)

Haman
Esther 3:5, 6

1. Their Work
   The wicked worketh a deceitful work: but to him that soweth righteousness shall be a sure reward. Proverbs 11:18
2. Their Counsel
   The thoughts of the righteous are right: but the counsels of the wicked are deceit. Proverbs 12:5

B. The False Witness

Jesus' Accusers
Mark 14:55-60

He that speaketh truth sheweth forth righteousness: but a false witness deceit. Proverbs 12:17

C. The Fool

Pharaoh
Exodus 8:28-29

The wisdom of the prudent is to understand his way: but the folly of fools is deceit. Proverbs 14:8

D. The Enemy

Judas
Mark 14:43-46

Faithful are the wounds of a friend; but the kisses of an enemy are deceitful. Proverbs 27:6

III. Consequences of the Deceitful Man

A. There Is an Aftertaste to His Deceit

Bread of deceit is sweet to a man; but afterwards his mouth shall be filled with gravel. Proverbs 20:17

B. His Wickedness Is Revealed

Whose hatred is covered by deceit, his wickedness shall be shewed before the whole congregation. Proverbs 26:26

Chapter 23

THE FAITHFUL MAN

Proverbs 28:20
A faithful man shall abound with
blessings: but he that maketh haste to
be rich shall not be innocent.

The dream of every employer is to employ the Faithful Man. A one-word definition of the Faithful Man is "trustworthy." He can be trusted to be on time, to be honest in his dealings, to work hard, and to finish the job. He can be depended upon without question. He strives for consistency in every aspect of his life.

Proverbs 20:6 says, "Most men will proclaim every one his own goodness: but a faithful man who can find?" Though the Faithful Man may be difficult to find, once he is found, he is highly valued.

The Faithful Man

Dictionary "FAITHFUL": Firm in adherence to the truth, and to the duties of religion.

Hebrew "FAITHFUL": Established, trustworthiness (529); firmness, security, truth (530).

I. Actions of the Faithful Man
A. Keeps Quiet What Is Told in Confidence

Jeremiah
(From the King)
Jeremiah 38:24-28

A talebearer revealeth secrets: but he that is of a faithful spirit concealeth the matter. Proverbs 11:13

B. Tells the Truth

Micaiah
I Kings 22:13-28

A faithful witness will not lie: but a false witness will utter lies. Proverbs 14:5

II. Characteristics of the Faithful Man
A. Is Trustworthy

Joseph
Genesis 39:2-6,
22-23

A wicked messenger falleth into mischief: but a faithful ambassador is health. Proverbs 13:17

B. Is Refreshing to His Master

Daniel
Daniel 6:3-4

1. A wicked messenger falleth into mischief: but a faithful ambassador is health. Proverbs 13:17
2. As the cold of snow in the time of harvest, so is a faithful messenger to them that send him: for he refresheth the soul of his masters.
Proverbs 25:13

III. Reward of the Faithful Man
He Will Abound with Blessings

A faithful man shall abound with blessings: but he that maketh haste to be rich shall not be innocent.
Proverbs 28:20

Chapter 24

THE HAPPY MAN

Proverbs 3:13
Happy is the man that findeth
wisdom, and the man that getteth
understanding.

The Happy Man is refreshing to those around him. His positive outlook naturally finds the good in people. True happiness can only come from serving Jesus. The actions of the Happy Man are all a direct result of obeying the Bible. God's desire is for all of us to be happy. His Word clearly shows us the recipe for happiness.

It is a comfort to know that God cannot lie, therefore His Word is also true. Christians have known for a long time that "A merry heart doeth good like a medicine: . . ." Proverbs 17:22. Doctors have now proven that humor helps the body. A Happy Man brings health to himself as well as to others.

The Happy Man

Dictionary "HAPPY": An enjoyable sensation from the possession of good.

Hebrew "HAPPY": Happiness, blessed (835).

I. Actions of the Happy Man
A. Finds Wisdom

Solomon
1 Kings 10:7-9

> Happy is the man that findeth wisdom, and the man that getteth understanding. Proverbs 3:13

B. Keeps Wisdom

Job
Job 28:28
Job 42:10-17

> She is a tree of life to them that lay hold upon her: and happy is every one that retaineth her. Proverbs 3:18
> Dictionary "RETAINETH": to sustain, to keep fast, obtain.

C. Shows Kindness to the Poor

Zacchaeus
Luke 19:6, 8, 9

> He that despiseth his neighbour sinneth: but he that hath mercy on the poor, happy is he. Proverbs 14:21

D. Trusts in the Lord

Philippian Jailor
Acts 16:30-34

> He that handleth a matter wisely shall find good:
> and whoso trusteth in the LORD, happy is he.
> Proverbs 16:20

E. Fears the Lord Always

Peter
Acts 5:29-33,
40-42

> Happy is the man that feareth alway: but he that
> hardeneth his heart shall fall into mischief.
> Proverbs 28:14

F. Keeps the Law

David
I Chronicles 15:13, 25

> Where there is no vision, the people perish: but he
> that keepeth the law, happy is he. Proverbs 29:18

II. Rewards of the Happy Man
A. Has a Cheerful Face

> A merry heart maketh a cheerful countenance:
> but by sorrow of the heart the spirit is broken.
> Proverbs 15:13

B. Has Good Health

> A merry heart doeth good like a medicine:
> but a broken spirit drieth the bones.
> Proverbs 17:22

Chapter 25

THE MERCIFUL MAN

Proverbs 11:17
The merciful man doeth good to his
own soul: but he that is cruel
troubleth his own flesh.

The Hebrew definition is the best description of the Merciful Man. The definition is "one who stoops or bends in kindness to an inferior." God is the greatest example of mercy, and He also expects His children to develop that characteristic. God gave His only begotten Son to die for a whole world of inferiors. How can Christians do less than show kindness to others?

The Merciful Man will help the poor. He is willing to give what he has to make the lives of others more comfortable even though he may have to take a loss. There is no division of the classes for the Merciful Man. To him, all men are human beings created by God.

The Merciful Man will have great blessing, if he holds to the truth. There is an old saying that states, "Mercy without truth is compromise, and the truth without mercy is cruelty." With a balance of mercy and truth a Christian can find favour with God and man (Proverbs 3:3, 4). This is quite a promise!

The Merciful Man

Dictionary "MERCY": That benevolence, mildness, or tenderness of heart, which causes a person to overlook injuries, or to treat an offender better that he deserves.

Hebrew "MERCY": Bend or stoop in kindness to an inferior (2603); kindness (2617).

I. Actions of the Merciful Man
A. Is Good to Himself

Mordecai
Esther 2:21-23;
6:1-11

> The merciful man doeth good to his own soul: but he that is cruel troubleth his own flesh.
> Proverbs 11:17

B. Helps the Poor

Good Samaritan
Luke 10:33-37

1. He that despiseth his neighbour sinneth: but he that hath mercy on the poor, happy is he. Proverbs 14:21
2. He that oppresseth the poor reproacheth his Maker: but he that honoureth him hath mercy on the poor. Proverbs 14:31

II. Characteristic of the Merciful Man
Is "Not Cruel"

David
I Samuel 25:21-35

> The merciful man doeth good to his own soul: but he that is cruel troubleth his own flesh.
> Proverbs 11:17

III. Rewards of the Merciful Man (with a balance of mercy and truth)

A. Favour and Good Understanding Are Found

Let not mercy and truth forsake thee: bind them about thy neck; write them upon the table of thine heart: So shalt thou find favour and good understanding in the sight of God and man. Proverbs 3:3, 4

B. Sin Is Purged

By mercy and truth iniquity is purged: and by the fear of the LORD men depart from evil. Proverbs 16:6

C. Leadership Is Preserved

Mercy and truth preserve the king: and his throne is upholden by mercy. Proverbs 20:28

IV. Way to Get Mercy

Devise Good

Do they not err that devise evil? but mercy and truth shall be to them that devise good. Proverbs 14:22

Chapter 26

THE UNDERSTANDING MAN

Proverbs 15:21
Folly is joy to him that is destitute of
wisdom: but a man of understanding
walketh uprightly.

The Man of Understanding has the ability to comprehend the principles of God's Word and how they apply to him. He takes knowledge and separates it mentally until he understands. A student can go to school, take algebra and make straight A's; but if he did not understand it, the "knowledge" of algebra cannot help him down the road. Proverbs 14:6 says, " . . . knowledge is easy unto him that understandeth." It is only after a child understands that he will learn. Until he understands that fire is hot, he will not stay away from it.

Understanding is part of the Proverb's formula for wisdom. Knowledge + Understanding = Wisdom. Knowledge is the facts. Understanding is comprehending those facts, and most importantly, wisdom is using those facts.

The Understanding Man

Dictionary "UNDERSTANDING": To have just and adequate ideas of; to comprehend.

Hebrew "UNDERSTANDING": Intelligence (8394); to separate mentally (995); the heart (3820).

I. Actions of the Man of Understanding
A. Listens to Counsel

Apollos
Acts 18:24-28

A wise man will hear, and will increase learning; and a man of understanding shall attain unto wise counsels: Proverbs 1:5

B. Is Slow to Wrath

Jeremiah
Jeremiah 28:10-17

He that is slow to wrath is of great understanding: but he that is hasty of spirit exalteth folly. Proverbs 14:29

C. Seeks Knowledge

Timothy
II Timothy 3:14, 15

The heart of him that hath understanding seeketh knowledge: but the mouth of fools feedeth on foolishness. Proverbs 15:14

D.   Walks Uprightly

Solomon
I Kings 3:3-14

Folly is joy to him that is destitute of wisdom: but
a man of understanding walketh uprightly.
Proverbs 15:21

E.   Accepts Reproof

David
II Samuel 12:7-13

1.   He that refuseth instruction despiseth his own
soul: but he that heareth reproof getteth
understanding. Proverbs 15:32
2.   Smite a scorner, and the simple will beware: and
reprove one that hath understanding, and he will
understand knowledge. Proverbs 19:25

F.   Seeks the Lord

Daniel
Daniel 5:12; 6:1-10

Evil men understand not judgment: but they that
seek the LORD understand all things.
Proverbs 28:5

II. Characteristics of the Man of Understanding
A.   Has Knowledge of the Holy

Joseph
Genesis 41:15, 16

The fear of the LORD is the beginning of
wisdom: and the knowledge of the holy is
understanding. Proverbs 9:10

B. Shuts His Lips

Saul
I Samuel 10:26, 27

Even a fool, when he holdeth his peace, is counted wise: and he that shutteth his lips is esteemed a man of understanding. Proverbs 17:28

Chapter 27

THE EVIL WOMAN

Proverbs 6:24
To keep thee from the evil woman,
from the flattery of the tongue of a
strange woman.

The Evil Woman can be saved or lost. A saved person who is backslidden can and will act like the lost. The best definition of the evil person comes from Proverbs 2:12-15. The Evil Woman has the same characteristics as the Evil Man in these verses. They speak frowardly, leave the paths of uprightness, walk in the ways of darkness, rejoice to do evil, and delight in the frowardness of the wicked. You will notice in v. 13 that they *leave* the paths of uprightness, which gives the indication they were once there. An evil person is best pictured as a saved person who went the way of the world. When studying Proverbs, it is easy to see the difference between the sinful saved and the lost by the words "evil" and "wicked." "Wicked" in Proverbs is always referring to a lost person. An Evil Woman can look good on the outside, but be evil on the inside. Her heart makes her evil. What is in her heart eventually comes out, even though she tries to hide it from others (Mark 7:20-23).

The Evil Woman

Dictionary "EVIL": Any deviation of a moral agent from the rules of conduct prescribed to him by God, or by legitimate human authority.

Hebrew "EVIL": Bad or evil, wretchedness, wrong (7451).

I. Actions of the Evil Woman
A. She Plans Evil

Jezebel
I Kings 21:1-16

1. Do they not err that devise evil? but mercy and truth shall be to them that devise good. Proverbs 14:22
2. An ungodly man diggeth up evil: and in his lips there is as a burning fire. Proverbs 16:27
3. He that deviseth to do evil shall be called a mischievous person. Proverbs 24:8

B. She Speaks Evil

Herodias
Matthew 14:1-11

The heart of the righteous studieth to answer: but the mouth of the wicked poureth out evil things. Proverbs 15:28

C. She Does Evil

Athaliah
II Chronicles 22:10

My son, walk not thou in the way with them; refrain thy foot from their path: For their feet run to evil, and make haste to shed blood. Proverbs 1:15, 16

II. Characteristics of the Evil Woman

A. She Is Deceitful

Delilah
Judges 16:4-21

> Deceit is in the heart of them that imagine evil: but to the counsellors of peace is joy. Proverbs 12:20

B. She Is Foolish

Job's Wife
Job 2:9, 10

1. The desire accomplished is sweet to the soul: but it is abomination to fools to depart from evil. Proverbs 13:19
2. A wise man feareth, and departeth from evil: but the fool rageth, and is confident. Proverbs 14:16

C. She Is Ungodly

Gomer
Hosea 1:3; 2:1-6

> An ungodly man diggeth up evil: and in his lips there is as a burning fire. Proverbs 16:27

D. She Is Mischievous

Sapphira
Acts 5:1-10

> He that deviseth to do evil shall be called a mischievous person. Proverbs 24:8

E. She Does Not Fear God

Lot's Wife
Genesis 19:15-17, 26

> By mercy and truth iniquity is purged: and by

the fear of the LORD men depart from evil. Proverbs 16:6

III. Consequences of the Evil Woman

A. Dies

As righteousness tendeth to life: so he that pursueth evil pursueth it to his own death. Proverbs 11:19

B. Bows (humbled) before the Good

The evil bow before the good; and the wicked at the gates of the righteous. Proverbs 14:19

C. Falls into Her Own Pit

Whoso causeth the righteous to go astray in an evil way, he shall fall himself into his own pit: but the upright shall have good things in possession. Proverbs 28:10

IV. Warnings Against the Evil Woman

A. God's Word Is the Way to Escape Her

1. But whoso hearkeneth unto me shall dwell safely, and shall be quiet from fear of evil. Proverbs 1:33
2. For the commandment is a lamp; and the law is light; and reproofs of instruction are the way of life: To keep thee from the evil woman, from the flattery of the tongue of a strange woman. Proverbs 6:23, 24

B. We Should Shun Her

1. Be not wise in thine own eyes: fear the LORD, and depart from evil. Proverbs 3:7
2. Enter not into the path of the wicked, and go not in the way of evil men. Avoid it, pass not by it, turn from it, and pass away. Proverbs 4:14, 15
3. Turn not to the right hand nor to the left: remove thy foot from evil. Proverbs 4:27
4. A prudent man foreseeth the evil, and hideth himself: but the simple pass on, and are

punished. Proverbs 22:3

    5.   A prudent man foreseeth the evil, and hideth himself; but the simple pass on, and are punished. Proverbs 27:12

C.   Discipline Will Cleanse Her

The blueness of a wound cleanseth away evil: so do stripes the inward parts of the belly. Proverbs 20:30

Proverbs 2:16
To deliver thee from the strange
woman, even from the stranger which
flattereth with her words;

Chapter 28

THE STRANGE WOMAN

Proverbs 2:16
To deliver thee from the strange
woman, even from the stranger which
flattereth with her words;

The Strange Woman is often looked at as a harlot, and she most certainly can be a harlot. However, in reality, the Strange Woman is anyone who is not your wife. Though "strange" can mean adulterous and outlandish, it also means foreign or non-relative. Many a man has been tricked by the Strange Woman because he did not see her as an adulterous woman. The only one who should not be strange to you is your wife. Every man should remember that every woman is not adulterous; but every woman, except the one he marries, should be foreign to him.

The Strange Woman is also referred to or is known by a few other titles. They are "whorish," "adulterous," and "foolish." Saved and lost alike can be known as "Strange Women." The devil would like for us to think that the Bible is only speaking of the lost. There are more warnings about the Strange Woman in Proverbs than any other device of ruin for the young man. May we carefully consider her ways and her end!

The Strange Woman

Dictionary "STRANGE": Foreign; belonging to others.

Hebrew "STRANGE": (2141) to turn aside; hence to be a foreigner (5237) strange (foreign, non-relative, adulterous, different).

I. Actions of the Strange Woman
A. She Flatters with Her Words

Delilah
Judges 16:4-17

1. To deliver thee from the strange woman, even from the stranger which flattereth with her words; Proverbs 2:16
2. For the lips of a strange woman drop as an honeycomb, and her mouth is smoother than oil: Proverbs 5:3
3. To keep thee from the evil woman, from the flattery of the tongue of a strange woman. Proverbs 6:24
4. That they may keep thee from the strange woman, from the stranger which flattereth with her words. Proverbs 7:5
5. With her much fair speech she caused him to yield, with the flattering of her lips she forced him. Proverbs 7:21

B. She Forsakes the Guide of Her Youth

Dinah
Genesis 34:1-7

Which forsaketh the guide of her youth, and forgetteth the covenant of her God. Proverbs 2:17

C. She Forgets the Covenant of Her God

Aholah & Aholibah
Ezekiel 23:1-10, 35

> Which forsaketh the guide of her youth, and forgetteth the covenant of her God. Proverbs 2:17

D. She Attacks the Senses of a Man

Bathsheba
II Samuel 11:1-5

1. Taste
   > I have peace offerings with me; this day have I payed my vows. Proverbs 7:14
2. Hearing
   > Therefore came I forth to meet thee, diligently to seek thy face, and I have found thee. Proverbs 7:15
3. Sight
   > I have decked my bed with coverings of tapestry, with carved works, with fine linen of Egypt. Proverbs 7:16
4. Touch
   > I have decked my bed with coverings of tapestry, with carved works, with fine linen of Egypt. Proverbs 7:16
5. Smell
   > I have perfumed my bed with myrrh, aloes, and cinnamon. Proverbs 7:17

E. She Steals from a Man

Solomon's Wives
I Kings 11:1-8

1. His Honour
   a. Lest thou give thine honour unto others, and thy years unto the cruel: Proverbs 5:9
   b. A wound and dishonour shall he get; and his

177

reproach shall not be wiped away. Proverbs 6:33

2. His Years

    Lest thou give thine honour unto others, and thy years unto the cruel: Proverbs 5:9

3. His Wealth

    a. Lest strangers be filled with thy wealth; and thy labours be in the house of a stranger; Proverbs 5:10

    b. For by means of a whorish woman a man is brought to a piece of bread: and the adulteress will hunt for the precious life. Proverbs 6:26

4. His Labour

    Lest strangers be filled with thy wealth; and thy labours be in the house of a stranger; Proverbs 5:10

5. His Innocence

    So he that goeth in to his neighbour's wife; whosoever toucheth her shall not be innocent. Proverbs 6:29

6. His Reputation

    a. For by means of a whorish woman a man is brought to a piece of bread: and the adulteress will hunt for the precious life. Proverbs 6:26

    b. A wound and dishonour shall he get; and his reproach shall not be wiped away. Proverbs 6:33

II. Characteristics of the Strange Woman

A.   She Has Worldly Attire

Tamar
Genesis 38:13-26

And, behold, there met him a woman with the attire of an harlot, and subtil of heart. Proverbs 7:10

178

B. She Hides Her Heart

Lot's Daughter
Genesis 19:30-38

And, behold, there met him a woman with the attire of an harlot, and subtil of heart. Proverbs 7:10

C. She Is Loud

Jezebel
II Kings 9:30-37

1. (She is loud and stubborn; her feet abide not in her house: Proverbs 7:11
2. A foolish woman is clamorous: she is simple, and knoweth nothing. Proverbs 9:13

D. She Is Stubborn

Herodias
Mark 6:17-24

(She is loud and stubborn; her feet abide not in her house: Proverbs 7:11

E. She Does Not Stay at Home

Levite's Concubine
Judges 19:1-3

(She is loud and stubborn; her feet abide not in her house: Now is she without, now in the streets, and lieth in wait at every corner.) Proverbs 7:11, 12

F. She Handles a Man

Potiphar's Wife
Genesis 39:7-12

So she caught him, and kissed him, and with an impudent face said unto him, Proverbs 7:13

179

G. She Is Outspoken

Daughters of Moab
Numbers 25:1-3

So she caught him, and kissed him, and with an impudent face said unto him, Proverbs 7:13

H. She Is Deceitful

Woman of Samaria
John 4:16-18

Therefore came I forth to meet thee, diligently to seek thy face, and I have found thee. Proverbs 7:15

I. She Is Foolish

Two Harlots
1 Kings 3:16-27

A foolish woman is clamorous: she is simple, and knoweth nothing. Proverbs 9:13

J. She Is Simple

Adulterous Woman
John 8:3-11

A foolish woman is clamorous: she is simple, and knoweth nothing. Proverbs 9:13

K. She Accepts No Responsibility for Her Sin

Cozbi
Numbers 25:1-15

Such is the way of an adulterous woman; she eateth, and wipeth her mouth, and saith, I have done no wickedness. Proverbs 30:20

III. Consequences of the Strange Woman
A. Poison
But her end is bitter as wormwood, sharp as a twoedged sword. Proverbs 5:4
B. Death
1. For her house inclineth unto death, and her paths unto the dead. Proverbs 2:18
2. Her feet go down to death; her steps take hold on hell. Proverbs 5:5
3. For she hath cast down many wounded: yea, many strong men have been slain by her. Her house is the way to hell, going down to the chambers of death. Proverbs 7:26, 27
4. But he knoweth not that the dead are there; and that her guests are in the depths of hell. Proverbs 9:18
C. Hell
1. Her feet go down to death; her steps take hold on hell. Proverbs 5:5
2. For her house inclineth unto death, and her paths unto the dead. Proverbs 2:18
3. Her house is the way to hell, going down to the chambers of death. Proverbs 7:27
4. But he knoweth not that the dead are there; and that her guests are in the depths of hell. Proverbs 9:18
D. No Way to Return
None that go unto her return again, neither take they hold of the paths of life. Proverbs 2:19
E. Tears
And thou mourn at the last, when thy flesh and thy body are consumed, Proverbs 5:11
F. Destruction
1. But whoso committeth adultery with a woman lacketh understanding: he that doeth it destroyeth his own soul. Proverbs 6:32
2. He goeth after her straightway, as an ox goeth to the slaughter, or as a fool to the correction of the stocks; Proverbs 7:22

G. Wounds

1. A wound and dishonour shall he get; and his reproach shall not be wiped away. Proverbs 6:33
2. For she hath cast down many wounded: yea, many strong men have been slain by her. Proverbs 7:26

H. Dishonour

A wound and dishonour shall he get; and his reproach shall not be wiped away. Proverbs 6:33

I. Reproach

A wound and dishonour shall he get; and his reproach shall not be wiped away. Proverbs 6:33

J. A Trap

1. Till a dart strike through his liver; as a bird hasteth to the snare, and knoweth not that it is for his life. Proverbs 7:23
2. The mouth of strange women is a deep pit: he that is abhorred of the LORD shall fall therein. Proverbs 22:14
3. For a whore is a deep ditch; and a strange woman is a narrow pit. Proverbs 23:27

IV. Warnings about the Strange Woman

A. Remove Far from Her

Remove thy way far from her, and come not nigh the door of her house: Proverbs 5:8

B. Come Not Nigh the Door of Her House

Remove thy way far from her, and come not nigh the door of her house: Proverbs 5:8

C. Lust Not after Her Beauty

Lust not after her beauty in thine heart; neither let her take thee with her eyelids. Proverbs 6:25

D. Don't Let Her Take Thee with Her Eyelids

Lust not after her beauty in thine heart; neither let her take thee with her eyelids. Proverbs 6:25

E. Don't Let Her Take the Precious Life

1. For by means of a whorish woman a man is brought to a piece of bread: and the adulteress will hunt for the precious life. Proverbs 6:26

2. To call passengers who go right on their ways: Proverbs 9:15

F.   Don't Let Your Heart Decline to Her Ways

Let not thine heart decline to her ways, go not astray in her paths. Proverbs 7:25

Chapter 29

THE FOOLISH WOMAN

Proverbs 9:13
A foolish woman is clamorous: she is simple, and knoweth nothing.

God warns us against calling a man a fool (Matthew 5:22), but a person can act foolish. Proverbs 9:13 says, "A foolish woman is clamorous (loud): she is simple, and knoweth nothing." This can refer to either a believer or an unbeliever. The longer people are saved and growing in the knowledge of Jesus Christ, the less they will be acting foolish. A Foolish Woman is known by the crowd with whom she runs (Proverbs 13:20). She is the direct opposite of the Wise Woman. She will be silly in word and deed.

The first thing to do to keep from being foolish is to be saved. The second is to read and practice the Bible, particularly the book of Proverbs, which is known for its wisdom.

The Foolish Woman

Dictionary "FOOLISH": One who is destitute of reason. One who follows his own inclinations.

Hebrew "FOOLISH": Fat; stupid, or silly (3684).

I. Actions of the Foolish Woman
A. She Does Mischief

Lot's Daughter
Genesis 19:31-38

It is as sport to a fool to do mischief: but a man of understanding hath wisdom. Proverbs 10:23

B. She Refuses Correction

Naomi
Ruth 1:1-21

1. The fear of the LORD is the beginning of knowledge: but fools despise wisdom and instruction. Proverbs 1:7
2. And, behold, there met him a woman with the attire of an harlot, and subtil of heart. Proverbs 7:10
3. Though thou shouldest bray a fool in a mortar among wheat with a pestle, yet will not his foolishness depart from him. Proverbs 27:22

C. She Utters All Her Mind

Idle Woman
I Timothy 5:13

1. Even a fool, when he holdeth his peace, is counted wise: and he that shutteth his lips is esteemed a man of understanding. Proverbs 17:28
2. A fool hath no delight in understanding, but that his heart may discover itself. Proverbs 18:2

3. A fool uttereth all his mind: but a wise man keepeth it in till afterwards. Proverbs 29:11

D. She Causes Strife

Peninnah
I Samuel 1:4-8

It is an honour for a man to cease from strife: but every fool will be meddling. Proverbs 20:3

E. She Despises Wisdom

Lot's Wife
Genesis 19:15-17, 26

1. The fear of the LORD is the beginning of knowledge: but fools despise wisdom and instruction. Proverbs 1:7
2. Speak not in the ears of a fool: for he will despise the wisdom of thy words. Proverbs 23:9

F. She Hates Knowledge

Eve
Genesis 2:16-17;
3:4-7

1. How long, ye simple ones, will ye love simplicity? and the scorners delight in their scorning, and fools hate knowledge?
Proverbs 1:22
2. The lips of the wise disperse knowledge: but the heart of the foolish doeth not so. Proverbs 15:7

G. She Has Loud and Silly Speech

Jezebel
II Kings 9:30-37

1. A foolish woman is clamorous: she is simple, and knoweth nothing. Proverbs 9:13

187

2. The wise in heart will receive commandments: but a prating fool shall fall. Proverbs 10:8
3. He that winketh with the eye causeth sorrow: but a prating fool shall fall. Proverbs 10:10
4. A prudent man concealeth knowledge: but the heart of fools proclaimeth foolishness. Proverbs 12:23
5. The tongue of the wise useth knowledge aright: but the mouth of fools poureth out foolishness. Proverbs 15:2
6. The heart of him that hath understanding seeketh knowledge: but the mouth of fools feedeth on foolishness. Proverbs 15:14

H. She Destroys Her Own House

Rebekah
Genesis 27:6-13, 41-46

Every wise woman buildeth her house: but the foolish plucketh it down with her hands. Proverbs 14:1

I. She Hides Her Hatred

Noadiah
Nehemiah 6:10-14

He that hideth hatred with lying lips, and he that uttereth a slander, is a fool. Proverbs 10:18

J. She Utters Slander

Miriam
Numbers 12:1-15

He that hideth hatred with lying lips, and he that uttereth a slander, is a fool. Proverbs 10:18

K.   She Laughs at Sin

Potiphar's Wife
   Genesis 39:7-12

   1.   Fools make a mock at sin: but among the
        righteous there is favour. Proverbs 14:9
   2.   Folly is joy to him that is destitute of wisdom: but
        a man of understanding walketh uprightly.
        Proverbs 15:21

L.   She Trusts in Her Own Heart

Orpah
   Ruth 1:8-15

        He that trusteth in his own heart is a fool: but
        whoso walketh wisely, he shall be delivered.
        Proverbs 28:26

M.   She Lifts Herself Up

Athaliah
   II Chronicles 22:10-12

   1.   In the mouth of the foolish is a rod of pride: but the
        lips of the wise shall preserve them.
        Proverbs 14:3
   2.   If thou hast done foolishly in lifting up thyself, or
        if thou hast thought evil, lay thine hand upon thy
        mouth. Proverbs 30:32

II.   Characteristics of the Foolish Woman
A.   Her Way Is Right in Her Own Eyes

Micah's Mother
   Judges 17:1-6

        The way of a fool is right in his own eyes: but he
        that hearkeneth unto counsel is wise.
        Proverbs 12:15

B.   She Makes Her Anger Known

Zipporah
Exodus 4:24-26

1.   A fool's wrath is presently known: but a prudent man covereth shame. Proverbs 12:16
2.   A stone is heavy, and the sand weighty; but a fool's wrath is heavier than them both. Proverbs 27:3

C.   She Makes Her Foolishness Known

Job's Wife
Job 2:9, 10

1.   Every prudent man dealeth with knowledge: but a fool layeth open his folly. Proverbs 13:16
2.   Wisdom resteth in the heart of him that hath understanding: but that which is in the midst of fools is made known. Proverbs 14:33

D.   She Makes No Effort to Depart from Evil

Rachel
Genesis 31:19, 30-35

1.   The desire accomplished is sweet to the soul: but it is abomination to fools to depart from evil. Proverbs 13:19
2.   The simple believeth every word: but the prudent man looketh well to his going. Proverbs 14:15

E.   She Has No Desire for Wisdom

Solomon's Wives
I Kings 11:1-8

1.   Wherefore is there a price in the hand of a fool to get wisdom, seeing he hath no heart to it? Proverbs 17:16

2. Wisdom is before him that hath understanding; but the eyes of a fool are in the ends of the earth. Proverbs 17:24
3. A fool hath no delight in understanding, but that his heart may discover itself. Proverbs 18:2
4. Wisdom is too high for a fool: he openeth not his mouth in the gate. Proverbs 24:7

F. She Is a Grief to Her Parents

Judith & Bashemath
Genesis 26:34, 35

He that begetteth a fool doeth it to his sorrow: and the father of a fool hath no joy. Proverbs 17:21

G. She Will Not Keep the Honour Given to Her

Michal
II Samuel 6:14-23

As he that bindeth a stone in a sling, so is he that giveth honour to a fool. Proverbs 26:8

H. She Is Simple

Dinah
Genesis 34:1-5

A foolish woman is clamorous: she is simple, and knoweth nothing. Proverbs 9:13

I. She Is Repeatedly Silly

Sarah
Genesis 12:10-20;
20:1-18

As a dog returneth to his vomit, so a fool returneth to his folly. Proverbs 26:11

J.   She Is Not Known for Having Excellent Speech

Witch of Endor

I Samuel 28:7-19

> Excellent speech becometh not a fool: much less do lying lips a prince. Proverbs 17:7

III. Consequences of the Foolish Woman

A.   Servanthood

> He that troubleth his own house shall inherit the wind: and the fool shall be servant to the wise of heart. Proverbs 11:29

B.   Contention

> A fool's lips enter into contention, and his mouth calleth for strokes. Proverbs 18:6

C.   Destruction

1.   Wise men lay up knowledge: but the mouth of the foolish is near destruction. Proverbs 10:14

2.   He that walketh with wise men shall be wise: but a companion of fools shall be destroyed. Proverbs 13:20

3.   A fool's mouth is his destruction, and his lips are the snare of his soul. Proverbs 18:7

D.   The Rod

1.   Judgments are prepared for scorners, and stripes for the back of fools. Proverbs 19:29

2.   A whip for the horse, a bridle for the ass, and a rod for the fool's back. Proverbs 26:3

E.   A Fall

1.   The wise in heart will receive commandments: but a prating fool shall fall. Proverbs 10:8

2.   He that winketh with the eye causeth sorrow: but a prating fool shall fall. Proverbs 10:10

F.   Shame

> The wise shall inherit glory: but shame shall be the promotion of fools. Proverbs 3:35

G.   Correction

> He goeth after her straightway, as an ox goeth to the slaughter, or as a fool to the correction of the

stocks; Proverbs 7:22

H. Death

The lips of the righteous feed many: but fools die for want of wisdom. Proverbs 10:21

I. No Honour

1. As snow in summer, and as rain in harvest, so honour is not seemly for a fool. Proverbs 26:1

2. As he that bindeth a stone in a sling, so is he that giveth honour to a fool. Proverbs 26:8

IV. Warning About the Foolish Woman

Forsake Her

Forsake the foolish, and live; and go in the way of understanding. Proverbs 9:6

Chapter 30

THE GOD-FEARING WOMAN

Proverbs 31:30
Favour is deceitful, and beauty is
vain: but a woman that feareth the
LORD, she shall be praised.

Very rarely do we hear someone say that a person is God-fearing. It used to be a term regularly used to compliment a person's character and their relationship with the Lord. Much is said of the fear of the Lord in Proverbs. The God-Fearing Woman has a reverential awe of God that causes her to live a life according to His will. She is a Christian with an outward glow of the Holy Spirit upon her.

The God-Fearing Woman

Dictionary "FEAR": In good men, the fear of God is a holy awe or reverence of God and His laws, which springs from a just view and real love of the divine character, leading the subjects of it to hate and shun every thing that can offend such a holy being and inclining them to aim at perfect obedience.

Hebrew "FEAR": Fear; morally reverence (3374).

I. Actions of a God-Fearing Woman
A. She Hates Evil

Vashti
Esther 1:10-12

1. Be not wise in thine own eyes: fear the LORD, and depart from evil. Proverbs 3:7
2. The fear of the LORD is to hate evil: pride, and arrogancy, and the evil way, and the froward mouth, do I hate. Proverbs 8:13
3. By mercy and truth iniquity is purged: and by the fear of the LORD men depart from evil. Proverbs 16:6

B. She Walks Uprightly

Elisabeth
Luke 1:5, 6

He that walketh in his uprightness feareth the LORD: but he that is perverse in his ways despiseth him. Proverbs 14:2

II. Characteristics of a God-Fearing Woman
A. She Has Knowledge

Deborah
Judges 4:4-5

The fear of the LORD is the beginning of knowledge: but fools despise wisdom and instruction. Proverbs 1:7

B. She Has Wisdom

Abigail
I Samuel 25:23-33

1. The fear of the LORD is the beginning of wisdom: and the knowledge of the holy is understanding. Proverbs 9:10
2. A wise man feareth, and departeth from evil: but the fool rageth, and is confident. Proverbs 14:16
3. The fear of the LORD is the instruction of wisdom; and before honour is humility. Proverbs 15:33

C. She Has Consistency

Anna
Luke 2:36-38

My son, fear thou the LORD and the king: and meddle not with them that are given to change: Proverbs 24:21

III. Rewards of a God-Fearing Woman
A. Prolonged Life

The fear of the LORD prolongeth days: but the years of the wicked shall be shortened. Proverbs 10:27

B. Strong Confidence

In the fear of the LORD is strong confidence: and his children shall have a place of refuge. Proverbs 14:26

C. Satisfaction

The fear of the LORD tendeth to life: and he that hath it shall abide satisfied; he shall not be visited with evil. Proverbs 19:23

D. Praise

> Favour is deceitful, and beauty is vain: but a woman that feareth the LORD, she shall be praised. Proverbs 31:30

E. Rewards

1. Whoso despiseth the word shall be destroyed: but he that feareth the commandment shall be rewarded. Proverbs 13:13
2. By humility and the fear of the LORD are riches, and honour, and life. Proverbs 22:4

F. Health

1. The fear of the LORD is a fountain of life, to depart from the snares of death. Proverbs 14:27
2. The fear of the LORD tendeth to life: and he that hath it shall abide satisfied; he shall not be visited with evil. Proverbs 19:23

Chapter 31

THE ANGRY WOMAN

Proverbs 21:19
It is better to dwell in the wilderness,
than with a contentious and an
angry woman.

The Angry Woman is often exposed too late. A man marries, seeing only the mild side of her quarrelsome personality. A girl often takes on the traits of her mother as is mentioned in Ezekiel 16:44. For instance, if a girl's mother has a bad temper, then she will have the tendency to have a bad temper as well. The only two things that can keep a girl from taking on the bad traits of her mother are: being born again, and being filled with the Spirit. Anger is a work of the flesh and is seen more readily when a person is not walking in the Spirit.

The Angry Woman

Dictionary "BRAWLING": To quarrel noisily and indecently.

Hebrew "BRAWLING": Brawling, contention (-ous) (4079).

Dictionary "CONTENTIOUS": Given to angry debate; quarrelsome.

Hebrew "CONTENTIOUS": A quarrel, strife, debate (4683).

Dictionary "ANGRY": A violent passion of the mind excited by a real or supposed injury; usually accompanied with a propensity to take vengeance, or to obtain satisfaction from the offending party.

Hebrew "ANGRY": The nose or nostril, hence the face, anger, wrath (639).

I. Actions of an Angry Woman
A. She Deals Foolishly

Herodias
Matthew 14:3-10

1. A fool's wrath is presently known: but a prudent man covereth shame. Proverbs 12:16
2. He that is soon angry dealeth foolishly: and a man of wicked devices is hated. Proverbs 14:17
3. He that is slow to wrath is of great understanding: but he that is hasty of spirit exalteth folly. Proverbs 14:29
4. A stone is heavy, and the sand weighty; but a fool's wrath is heavier than them both. Proverbs 27:3

B.   She Stirs up Strife

Rachel
  Genesis 29:32-30:2

> As coals are to burning coals, and wood to fire; so is a contentious man to kindle strife. Proverbs 26:21

C.   She Speaks Grievous Words

Sarah
  Genesis 21:9-12

> A soft answer turneth away wrath: but grievous words stir up anger. Proverbs 15:1

II.   Characteristics of an Angry Woman

A.   She Is Hard to Live With

Michal
  II Samuel 6:14-23

1.   It is better to dwell in a corner of the housetop, than with a brawling woman in a wide house. Proverbs 21:9
2.   It is better to dwell in the corner of the housetop, than with a brawling woman and in a wide house. Proverbs 25:24

B.   Her Contention Is Continual

Peninnah
  I Samuel 1:2-7

1.   A fool's lips enter into contention, and his mouth calleth for strokes. Proverbs 18:6
2.   A foolish son is the calamity of his father: and the contentions of a wife are a continual dropping. Proverbs 19:13
3.   A continual dropping in a very rainy day and a contentious woman are alike. Proverbs 27:15

C. She Does Not Rule Her Spirit

Athaliah
II Chronicles 23:12-15

> He that is slow to anger is better than the mighty; and he that ruleth his spirit than he that taketh a city. Proverbs 16:32

D. Her Contention Is Caused by Pride

Miriam
Numbers 12:1-15

> Only by pride cometh contention: but with the well advised is wisdom. Proverbs 13:10

E. She Is a Scorner

Jezebel
I Kings 19:1, 2

> Cast out the scorner, and contention shall go out; yea, strife and reproach shall cease. Proverbs 22:10

III. Consequences of the Angry Woman

A. People Want to Get Away from Her

> It is better to dwell in the wilderness, than with a contentious and an angry woman. Proverbs 21:19

B. People Want to Hide Her

> A continual dropping in a very rainy day and a contentious woman are alike. Whosoever hideth her hideth the wind, and the ointment of his right hand, which bewrayeth itself. Proverbs 27:15, 16

C. People Want to Smite Her

> A fool's lips enter into contention, and his mouth calleth for strokes. Proverbs 18:6

Chapter 32

THE VIRTUOUS WOMAN

Proverbs 12:4
A virtuous woman is a crown to
her husband: but she that maketh
ashamed is as rottenness in his bones.

Every woman should have the goal of being a Virtuous Woman. She is the example of moral excellence in character, in personality, in love, and in diligence. Because a Virtuous Women is hard to find, she stands out (Proverbs 31:10). God devotes almost an entire chapter to the description of the Virtuous Woman. The Virtuous Woman is what every father desires in his daughter and every man desires in a wife. She will bring honor to her husband, glory to her father, and a good name to herself.

The Virtuous Woman

Dictionary "VIRTUOUS": Morally good; acting in conformity to the moral law; practicing the moral duties, and abstaining from vice.

Hebrew "VIRTUOUS": a force; wealth, virtue, valor, strength (2428).

I.   Actions of a Virtuous Woman
A.   She Seeks the Tools to Do a Job

Great Woman
Of Shunem
II Kings 4:8-10

> She seeketh wool, and flax, and worketh willingly with her hands. Proverbs 31:13

B.   She Works Willingly with Her Hands

Rebekah
Genesis 24:15-20

1.   She seeketh wool, and flax, and worketh willingly with her hands. Proverbs 31:13
2.   She considereth a field, and buyeth it: with the fruit of her hands she planteth a vineyard. She girdeth her loins with strength, and strengtheneth her arms. Proverbs 31:16, 17
3.   She layeth her hands to the spindle, and her hands hold the distaff. Proverbs 31:19

C.   She Helps the Poor and Needy

Phebe
Romans 16:1, 2

> She stretcheth out her hand to the poor; yea, she reacheth forth her hands to the needy.
> Proverbs 31:20

D.   She Does Good toward Her Husband

Abigail
I Samuel 25:2-33

> She will do him good and not evil all the days of her life. Proverbs 31:12

E.   She Sells What She Makes for a Profit

Lydia
Acts 16:14, 15

1.   She considereth a field, and buyeth it: with the fruit of her hands she planteth a vineyard. Proverbs 31:16
2.   She perceiveth that her merchandise is good: her candle goeth not out by night. Proverbs 31:18
3.   She maketh fine linen, and selleth it; and delivereth girdles unto the merchant. Proverbs 31:24

F.   She Speaks with Wisdom and Kindness

Lemuel's Mother
Proverbs 31:1-9

> She openeth her mouth with wisdom; and in her tongue is the law of kindness. Proverbs 31:26

G.   She Looks after Her Household

Esther
Esther 4:13-16

> She looketh well to the ways of her household, and eateth not the bread of idleness. Proverbs 31:27

II. Characteristics of the Virtuous Woman
A. She Is a Crown to Her Husband

Priscilla
Acts 18:2, 18, 26
Romans 16:3, 4

1. A virtuous woman is a crown to her husband: but she that maketh ashamed is as rottenness in his bones. Proverbs 12:4
2. Her husband is known in the gates, when he sitteth among the elders of the land. Proverbs 31:23

B. She Is of More Value than Rubies

Ruth
Ruth 3:11

Who can find a virtuous woman? for her price is far above rubies. Proverbs 31:10

C. She Is Trusted by Her Husband

Mary
Matthew 1:18-25

The heart of her husband doth safely trust in her, so that he shall have no need of spoil. Proverbs 31:11

D. She Meets the Needs of Others, at the Sacrifice of Herself

Widow of Zarephath
I Kings 17:8-16

She riseth also while it is yet night, and giveth meat to her household, and a portion to her maidens. Proverbs 31:15

E. She Is a Strong Woman

Jael
Judges 4:16-22

1. She girdeth her loins with strength, and strengtheneth her arms. Proverbs 31:17
2. Strength and honour are her clothing; and she shall rejoice in time to come. Proverbs 31:25

F. She Is Prepared

Wise Virgins
Matthew 25:1-13

She perceiveth that her merchandise is good: her candle goeth not out by night. Proverbs 31:18

G. She Sews

Dorcas
Acts 9:36-43

1. She layeth her hands to the spindle, and her hands hold the distaff. Proverbs 31:19
2. She maketh herself coverings of tapestry; her clothing is silk and purple. Proverbs 31:22
3. She maketh fine linen, and selleth it; and delivereth girdles unto the merchant. Proverbs 31:24

H. She Keeps Her Family Clothed

Hannah
1 Samuel 2:18-21

She is not afraid of the snow for her household: for all her household are clothed with scarlet. Proverbs 31:21

I. **She Keeps Herself Looking Presentable**

Vashti
Esther 1:10-12

She maketh herself coverings of tapestry; her clothing is silk and purple. Proverbs 31:22

J. **She Is Not Lazy**

Anna
Luke 2:36-38

She looketh well to the ways of her household, and eateth not the bread of idleness. Proverbs 31:27

K. **She Fears the Lord**

Shiphrah & Puah
Exodus 1:15-21

Favour is deceitful, and beauty is vain: but a woman that feareth the LORD, she shall be praised. Proverbs 31:30

III. Rewards of the Virtuous Woman
A. Strength
Strength and honour are her clothing; and she shall rejoice in time to come. Proverbs 31:25
B. Honour
Strength and honour are her clothing; and she shall rejoice in time to come. Proverbs 31:25
C. Joy
Strength and honour are her clothing; and she shall rejoice in time to come. Proverbs 31:25
D. Praise
1. Her children arise up, and call her blessed; her husband also, and he praiseth her. Proverbs 31:28
2. Favour is deceitful, and beauty is vain: but a woman that feareth the LORD, she shall be

praised. Proverbs 31:30

3. Give her of the fruit of her hands; and let her own works praise her in the gates. Proverbs 31:31

Chapter 33

THE WISE WOMAN

Proverbs 14:1
Every wise woman buildeth her
house: but the foolish plucketh it
down with her hands.

Wisdom is the primary subject of Proverbs. The Wise Woman learns knowledge, exercises understanding, and applies wisdom. Jesus is wisdom personified, so the truly Wise Woman is a believer. Her increase of wisdom comes from the Word of God. She is willing to learn from others and to accept reproof. She is notable because it is easier to be foolish than to be wise. The Wise Woman is highly treasured and in high demand.

The Wise Woman

Dictionary "WISE": Properly having knowledge; hence having the power of discerning and judging correctly, or of discriminating between what is true and what is false. It is the discrete use or application of knowledge.

Hebrew "WISE": To be wise in mind, word, or act (2499) Note: Knowledge + Understanding = Wisdom (Proverbs 2:6).

I.   Actions of the Wise Woman
A.   She Works Hard

Ruth
Ruth 2:1-7

Go to the ant, thou sluggard; consider her ways, and be wise: Proverbs 6:6

B.   She Receives Instruction

Queen of Sheba
1 Kings 10:1-9

1. Hear instruction, and be wise, and refuse it not. Proverbs 8:33
2. The wise in heart will receive commandments: but a prating fool shall fall. Proverbs 10:8
3. The heart of the wise teacheth his mouth, and addeth learning to his lips. Proverbs 16:23
4. The heart of the prudent getteth knowledge; and the ear of the wise seeketh knowledge. Proverbs 18:15
5. Hear counsel, and receive instruction, that thou mayest be wise in thy latter end. Proverbs 19:20
6. When the scorner is punished, the simple is made wise: and when the wise is instructed, he receiveth knowledge. Proverbs 21:11
7. Hear thou, my son, and be wise, and guide thine heart in the way. Proverbs 23:19

C. She Accepts Reproof

Sarah
Genesis 20:9-18

1. The ear that heareth the reproof of life abideth among the wise. Proverbs 15:31
2. The rod and reproof give wisdom: but a child left to himself bringeth his mother to shame. Proverbs 29:15

D. She Refrains from Speaking

Esther
Esther 5:1-8; 7:1-6

In the multitude of words there wanteth not sin: but he that refraineth his lips is wise. Proverbs 10:19

E. She Listens to Counsel

Bathsheba
1 Kings 1:10-31

1. The way of a fool is right in his own eyes: but he that hearkeneth unto counsel is wise. Proverbs 12:15
2. Only by pride cometh contention: but with the well advised is wisdom. Proverbs 13:10
3. Hear counsel, and receive instruction, that thou mayest be wise in thy latter end. Proverbs 19:20

F. She Obeys Her Parents

Daughters of
Phillip
Acts 21:8, 9

The father of the righteous shall greatly rejoice: and he that begetteth a wise child shall have joy of him. Proverbs 23:24

G. She Fears the Lord

Shiphrah & Puah
Exodus 1:15-21

1. The fear of the LORD is the beginning of wisdom: and the knowledge of the holy is understanding. Proverbs 9:10
2. The fear of the LORD is the instruction of wisdom; and before honour is humility. Proverbs 15:33

II. Characteristics of the Wise Woman
A. She Is Wise in Heart

Wise Woman
Of Abel
II Samuel 20:16-22

He that troubleth his own house shall inherit the wind: and the fool shall be servant to the wise of heart. Proverbs 11:29

B. She Wins Souls

Anna
Luke 2:36-38

The fruit of the righteous is a tree of life; and he that winneth souls is wise. Proverbs 11:30

C. She Speaks Healing Words

Wise Woman
of Tekoah
II Samuel 14:2-21

1. There is that speaketh like the piercings of a sword: but the tongue of the wise is health. Proverbs 12:18
2. She openeth her mouth with wisdom; and in her tongue is the law of kindness. Proverbs 31:26

D. She Builds Her House

Eunice
II Timothy 1:5; 3:14, 15

1. Every wise woman buildeth her house: but the foolish plucketh it down with her hands. Proverbs 14:1
2. Through wisdom is an house builded; and by understanding it is established: Proverbs 24:3

E. She Is Humble

Sinful Woman
Luke 7:36-50

1. When pride cometh, then cometh shame: but with the lowly is wisdom. Proverbs 11:2
2. In the mouth of the foolish is a rod of pride: but the lips of the wise shall preserve them. Proverbs 14:3

F. She Is a Servant

Tabitha
Acts 9:36-41

The king's favour is toward a wise servant: but his wrath is against him that causeth shame. Proverbs 14:35

G. She Speaks with Knowledge

Huldah
II Kings 22:14-20

1. The tongue of the wise useth knowledge aright: but the mouth of fools poureth out foolishness. Proverbs 15:2
2. The lips of the wise disperse knowledge: but the heart of the foolish doeth not so. Proverbs 15:7

H. She Is Prudent

Deborah
Judges 4:4-24

1. I wisdom dwell with prudence, and find out knowledge of witty inventions. Proverbs 8:12
2. The wisdom of the prudent is to understand his way: but the folly of fools is deceit. Proverbs 14:8
3. The wise in heart shall be called prudent: and the sweetness of the lips increaseth learning. Proverbs 16:21

I. She Does Not Drink Alcohol

Manoah's Wife
Judges 13:2-7, 14

Wine is a mocker, strong drink is raging: and whosoever is deceived thereby is not wise. Proverbs 20:1

J. She Is Not Wasteful

Mary of Bethany
Matthew 26:6-13

There is treasure to be desired and oil in the dwelling of the wise; but a foolish man spendeth it up. Proverbs 21:20

K. She Is Not a Respecter of Persons

Rebekah
Genesis 24:15-24

1. The mouth of the just bringeth forth wisdom: but the froward tongue shall be cut out. Proverbs 10:31
2. He that is void of wisdom despiseth his neighbour: but a man of understanding holdeth his peace. Proverbs 11:12

3. These things also belong to the wise. It is not good to have respect of persons in judgment. Proverbs 24:23

L. She Has an Understanding Heart

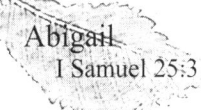
Abigail
1 Samuel 25:3

1. In the lips of him that hath understanding wisdom is found: but a rod is for the back of him that is void of understanding. Proverbs 10:13
2. It is as sport to a fool to do mischief: but a man of understanding hath wisdom. Proverbs 10:23
3. Wisdom resteth in the heart of him that hath understanding: but that which is in the midst of fools is made known. Proverbs 14:33
4. Wisdom is before him that hath understanding; but the eyes of a fool are in the ends of the earth. Proverbs 17:24

III. The Rewards of Being a Wise Woman
A. Glory
The wise shall inherit glory: but shame shall be the promotion of fools. Proverbs 3:35
B. Riches
1. For wisdom is better than rubies; and all the things that may be desired are not to be compared to it. Proverbs 8:11
2. The crown of the wise is their riches: but the foolishness of fools is folly. Proverbs 14:24
C. Protection
1. When wisdom entereth into thine heart, and knowledge is pleasant unto thy soul; Discretion shall preserve thee, understanding shall keep thee: Proverbs 2:10, 11
2. Get wisdom, get understanding: forget it not; neither decline from the words of my mouth. Forsake her not, and she shall preserve thee: love

her, and she shall keep thee. Proverbs 4:5, 6

3. He that trusteth in his own heart is a fool: but whoso walketh wisely, he shall be delivered. Proverbs 28:26

D. Happiness

Happy is the man that findeth wisdom, and the man that getteth understanding. Proverbs 3:13

E. Life

My son, let not them depart from thine eyes: keep sound wisdom and discretion: So shall they be life unto thy soul, and grace to thy neck. Proverbs 3:21, 22

F. Grace

1. My son, let not them depart from thine eyes: keep sound wisdom and discretion: So shall they be life unto thy soul, and grace to thy neck. Proverbs 3:21, 22

2. Wisdom is the principal thing; therefore get wisdom: and with all thy getting get understanding. Exalt her, and she shall promote thee: she shall bring thee to honour, when thou dost embrace her. She shall give to thine head an ornament of grace: a crown of glory shall she deliver to thee. Proverbs 4:7-9

G. Honor

Wisdom is the principal thing; therefore get wisdom: and with all thy getting get understanding. Exalt her, and she shall promote thee: she shall bring thee to honour, when thou dost embrace her. Proverbs 4:7, 8

H. Rewards

So shall the knowledge of wisdom be unto thy soul: when thou hast found it, then there shall be a reward, and thy expectation shall not be cut off. Proverbs 24:14

I. Good

1. If thou be wise, thou shalt be wise for thyself: but if thou scornest, thou alone shalt bear it. Proverbs 9:12

2. He that handleth a matter wisely shall find good: and whoso trusteth in the LORD, happy is he. Proverbs 16:20

3. He that getteth wisdom loveth his own soul: he that keepeth understanding shall find good. Proverbs 19:8

J. Joy to Parents

Whoso loveth wisdom rejoiceth his father: but he that keepeth company with harlots spendeth his substance. Proverbs 29:3

Chapter 34

THE PRUDENT WOMAN

Proverbs 19:14
House and riches are the inheritance
of fathers: and a prudent wife is from
the LORD.

Prudence is an important quality for men and women, but it is uniquely important for women. Prudence is a quality found in a good secretary, a good assistant, and especially a good wife. It is the ability to plan ahead in order to be prepared; prepared to handle temptation, to do a job, or to take care of a problem. One of the many ways a wife displays prudence is by planning a week's meals. For a school teacher, it is knowing what academic principle he or she wants to reach by the end of a week and working toward that goal. To sum it up, prudence is "thinking."

The Prudent Woman

Dictionary "PRUDENT": Cautious; circumspect; careful of the consequences, measures or action.

Hebrew "PRUDENT": Cunning (6175); to separate mentally (distinguish); beware; intelligent; guide wittingly; crafty; subtil (995).

I.   Actions of the Prudent Woman
A.   She Listens to Reproof

Esther
Esther 4:1-16

> A fool despiseth his father's instruction: but he that regardeth reproof is prudent. Proverbs 15:5

B.   She Gets Knowledge

Mary
Luke 10:38-42

> The heart of the prudent getteth knowledge; and the ear of the wise seeketh knowledge. Proverbs 18:15

II.   Characteristics of the Prudent Woman
A.   She Is Wise in Heart

Israelite Woman
Exodus 35:25, 26

> The wise in heart shall be called prudent: and the sweetness of the lips increaseth learning. Proverbs 16:21

B.   She Is a Gift from God

Rebekah
Genesis 24:14, 15, 50-58

House and riches are the inheritance of fathers:
and a prudent wife is from the LORD.
Proverbs 19:14

C. She Understands Her Way

Abigail
I Samuel 25:14-33

The wisdom of the prudent is to understand his
way: but the folly of fools is deceit.
Proverbs 14:8

III. Rewards of the Prudent Woman
A. She Is Crowned with Knowledge
1. The wisdom of the prudent is to understand his
   way: but the folly of fools is deceit.
   Proverbs 14:8
2. The heart of the prudent getteth knowledge; and
   the ear of the wise seeketh knowledge.
   Proverbs 18:15

B. She Has Wisdom
1. I wisdom dwell with prudence, and find out
   knowledge of witty inventions. Proverbs 8:12
2. The wisdom of the prudent is to understand his
   way: but the folly of fools is deceit.
   Proverbs 14:8
3. The wise in heart shall be called prudent: and the
   sweetness of the lips increaseth learning.
   Proverbs 16:21

Chapter 35

THE ODIOUS WOMAN

Proverbs 30:23
For an odious woman when she
is married; and an handmaid
that is heir to her mistress.

The Odious Woman is a hateful woman. She is critical, negative, and downright mean. She is hard to live with and not pleasant to be around. Her negative spirit makes those she is near miserable. The hatred in her heart comes out her lips and is shown by her actions. She cannot help but to do and to say what she feels. The end of such a woman is bitterness, which troubles her and defiles others. Hatred must be confessed and forsaken before it becomes a habit of life. No one likes a hateful woman!

The Odious Woman

Dictionary "ODIOUS": Hateful; deserving hatred; offensive to the senses; causing hate.

Hebrew "ODIOUS": (8130) To hate; enemy; foe.

I. Actions of the Odious Woman
A. Hates Knowledge

Lot's Wife
Genesis 19:15-17, 26

> How long, ye simple ones, will ye love simplicity? and the scorners delight in their scorning, and fools hate knowledge?
> Proverbs 1:22

B. Hates Reproof

Herodias
Mark 6:17-26

1. Whoso loveth instruction loveth knowledge: but he that hateth reproof is brutish. Proverbs 12:1
2. Correction is grievous unto him that forsaketh the way: and he that hateth reproof shall die. Proverbs 15:10

C. Covers Her Hatred with Deceit

Delilah
Judges 16:4-21

> He that hateth dissembleth with his lips, and layeth up deceit within him; When he speaketh fair, believe him not: for there are seven abominations in his heart. Whose hatred is covered by deceit, his wickedness shall be shewed before the whole congregation.
> Proverbs 26:24-26

D. Takes People Apart with Her Lips

Michal
II Samuel 6:16-23

> He that hateth dissembleth with his lips, and layeth up deceit within him; When he speaketh fair, believe him not: for there are seven abominations in his heart. Whose hatred is covered by deceit, his wickedness shall be shewed before the whole congregation.
> Proverbs 26:24-26

E. Lies

Jezebel
I Kings 21:7-16

1. He that hideth hatred with lying lips, and he that uttereth a slander, is a fool. Proverbs 10:18
2. A lying tongue hateth those that are afflicted by it; and a flattering mouth worketh ruin.
   Proverbs 26:28

II. Characteristics of the Odious Woman

A. She Has the Tendency of a Fool

Job's Wife
Job 2:9, 10

1. How long, ye simple ones, will ye love simplicity? and the scorners delight in their scorning, and fools hate knowledge?
   Proverbs 1:22
2. Whoso loveth instruction loveth knowledge: but he that hateth reproof is brutish. Proverbs 12:1

B. She Has the Tendency of a Scorner

Miriam
Numbers 12:1-15

Reprove not a scorner, lest he hate thee: rebuke a wise man, and he will love thee. Proverbs 9:8

C. She Has the Tendency of a Murderous Person

Athaliah
II Kings 11:1-3

The bloodthirsty hate the upright: but the just seek his soul. Proverbs 29:10

D. She Has the Tendency to Withhold Discipline

Nehushta
II Kings 24:8, 9

He that spareth his rod hateth his son: but he that loveth him chasteneth him betimes. Proverbs 13:24

E. She Has the Tendency to Hate the Poor

Zeresh
Esther 5:12-14

All the brethren of the poor do hate him: how much more do his friends go far from him? he pursueth them with words, yet they are wanting to him. Proverbs 19:7

III. Consequence of the Odious Woman
Strife

Hatred stirreth up strifes: but love covereth all sins. Proverbs 10:12

Chapter 36

THE GRACIOUS WOMAN

Proverbs 11:16
A gracious woman retaineth honour:
and strong men retain riches.

A Gracious Woman is well-liked. She is the recipient of praise, honor, and love. In reality, she reaps what she sows. The familiar Proverb, "A man that hath friends must shew himself friendly" (Proverbs 18:24) is the principle by which she lives her life. She is kind to the rich **and** the poor, to the intelligent **and** the ignorant, and to the young **and** the old. She is consistent in her attitudes and actions toward others. She tries to bestow the same grace or unmerited favor on others that she has been shown by God. She looks for ways to be a blessing to people, which results in self-sacrifice on her part. Though definitely a characteristic of a Virtuous Woman, God makes special mention of the woman who has *grace*.

The Gracious Woman

Dictionary "GRACIOUS": Favorable; kind; friendly; benevolent; merciful; expressing kindness and favor.

Hebrew "GRACIOUS": (2580) Graciousness, kindness, favor.

I. Action of the Gracious Woman
Speaks with Kindness

Abigail
1 Samuel 25:23-33

> He that loveth pureness of heart, for the grace of his lips the king shall be his friend.
> Proverbs 22:11

II. Characteristics of the Gracious Woman
A. She Is Wise

Rahab
Joshua 2:12-21

1. My son, let not them depart from thine eyes: keep sound wisdom and discretion: So shall they be life unto thy soul, and grace to thy neck. Proverbs 3:21, 22
2. Wisdom is the principal thing; therefore get wisdom: and with all thy getting get understanding. Exalt her, and she shall promote thee: she shall bring thee to honour, when thou dost embrace her. She shall give to thine head an ornament of grace: a crown of glory shall she deliver to thee. Proverbs 4:7-9

B.   She Is Humble

Surely he scorneth the scorners: but he giveth grace unto the lowly. Proverbs 3:34

C.   She Is Pure in Heart

He that loveth pureness of heart, for the grace of his lips the king shall be his friend.
Proverbs 22:11

D.   She Is Virtuous

1.   Who can find a virtuous woman? for her price is far above rubies. Proverbs 31:10
2.   She openeth her mouth with wisdom; and in her tongue is the law of kindness. Proverbs 31:26

III. Rewards of the Gracious Woman

A.   Honour

A gracious woman retaineth honour: and strong men retain riches. Proverbs 11:16

B.   Friends

He that loveth pureness of heart, for the grace of his lips the king shall be his friend.
Proverbs 22:11

Chapter 37

THE FAIR WOMAN

Proverbs 11:22
As a jewel of gold in a swine's snout,
so is a fair woman which is without
discretion.

It is a shame that Solomon gave so many warnings about women but gave into that very temptation himself. It should be a warning to us all that fair skin can take down any Christian. King Lemuel's mother warned him "Give not thy strength unto women,.." Proverbs 31:3. How easy it is to marry for the outward beauty instead of the inward virtue. The inward beauty always outlasts the outward beauty. I always tell our youth "as is the mother, so is the daughter." To get a picture of what you are marrying and what she will be like in twenty years, look at the girl's mother. Solomon closes Proverbs saying, "Favour is deceitful, and beauty is vain" 31:30; "vain" meaning empty. The man who married a pretty girl with no character did not get much. When time and children have taken away the fair skin, he will be sorry. If a man marries a girl for her strength of character, she can retain that all her days.

The Fair Woman

Dictionary "FAIR": Clear; beautiful; handsome; pleasing to the eye; clear; favorable.

Hebrew "FAIR": Beautiful. (3303).

Three Warnings About Fair Women
I. Beauty Should Not Be Lusted After
(Delighted in)

Bathsheba
II Samuel 11:2-4

> Lust not after her beauty in thine heart; neither let her take thee with her eyelids. Proverbs 6:25

II. Beauty without Discretion is Like a Jewel in a Pig's Nose

Daughter of
Herodias
Matthew 14:3-11

> As a jewel of gold in a swine's snout, so is a fair woman which is without discretion.
> Proverbs 11:22

III. Beauty Is an Empty Thing

Delilah
Judges 16:4-21

> Favour is deceitful, and beauty is vain: but a woman that feareth the LORD, she shall be praised. Proverbs 31:30

INDEX